First published in the UK by Sona Books, an imprint of Danann Media Publishing Limited

Original material reproduced by courtesy of Future Publishing/Rugby World 2023

CAT NO. SONO555

Written by Tom O'Neill , Alan Pearey with Cameron Thurlow
Cover design: Darren Grice
Book design: Paul Southcombe
Editor: Martin Corteel
Proof reader: Cameron Thurlow
Contributors: Alan Pearey, Charlie Morgan, Owain Jones, Katie Field, John Griffiths, Adam Hathaway, Alan Dymock, Iain Spragg

Cover images: Getty Images
Book images: Alamy, Getty images
Additional images:
Stefano Delfrate
Warwick Gastinger

Made in EU.

ISBN: 978-1-915343-15-4

RUGBY LEGENDS

MEET THE GREATEST RUGBY PLAYERS OF ALL TIME

GILBERT
ISUZU

RUGBY
WORLD CUP
JAPAN

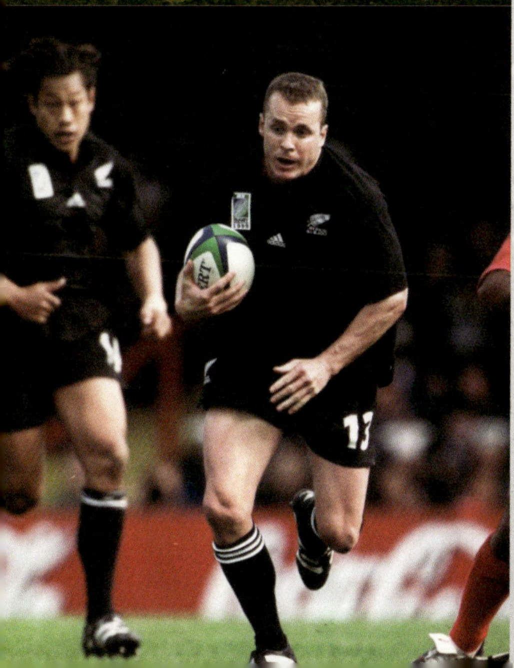

RUGBY LEGENDS

CONTENTS

INTRODUCTION

It's customary when choosing all-time greats from a cast of thousands to say how difficult a task it is, and how you're unlikely to agree with our selection. Both those statements are true, of course, and certainly we agonised over numerous positions.

We've touched on the greats from all the top rugby nations around the world, from long-gone eras of rugged Lions, the many times of All Black dominance, and some trailblazers of the modern game. But, as with any list, some big names have been left out. This book can provide you rugby lovers great debate: feel free to disagree, slander and pump fists in outrage. That's where the fun comes in.

But there are only limited numbers of slots per position, so something had to give. We make no apology for our choice of 127 players who were masters of their craft and shaped the history of the game. Indeed, through this list, you will be transported through the great teams and games of rugby history – enjoy.

RUGBY LEGENDS

FULL-BACKS

You need rare courage to be the rock at the rear, so any butter-fingered shrinking violets should step away now – full-backs need to spring like a hare and catch the ball unerringly in the face of dastardly challengers. Positional awareness is a given – you have a lot of ground to cover out there – and a solid boot is required to clear your lines. If you can also kick goals like Leigh Halfpenny, consider yourself hired. The best exponents of full-back play will pose endless threats as a runner, linking with their fellow backs or bursting into the line to create an overlap.

GAVIN HASTINGS

Braveheart Hastings captained Scotland on 20 occasions

MAJOR TEAMS: Watsonians, London Scottish, Cambridge University

Gavin Hastings was Scotland's granite-hard talisman for a decade, not only as the last line of defence but as a place kicker of unerring accuracy who often proved the difference between sides.

Earmarked for success from an early age, the Edinburgh-born Hastings attended George Watson's College before gaining his Cambridge Blue. First picked by Scotland in 1986, when he kicked six penalties to beat France 18-17, he was to lead his country on 20 occasions.

With brother Scott playing alongside him, 'Big Gav' loved to hit the line at speed, using his full 6ft 2in, 15st frame to bust defences. His power and ability to read the game brought him 17 Scotland tries and he notched 667 points in his Scotland career – at one point holding both his country's points record and the World Cup points record (227).

Position	Full-back
Country	Scotland
Test span	1986-95
Scotland caps	61 (61 starts)
Lions caps	6 (6 starts)
Test points	733 (18T, 87C, 160P)

He appeared in three World Cups, his biggest regret coming in the 1991 semi-final against England. With the scores tied, he missed an easy kick that would have put Scotland 9-6 ahead late on. On the flip side, his 21 points as Scotland handed the Auld Enemy their biggest loss in the 1986 fixture (33-6) is among his fondest memories.

Hastings was a mainstay of the 1989 Lions tour to Australia, and he went on to captain them in New Zealand in 1993, beating his old adversary Will Carling to the role. It led Sir Ian McGeechan to remark that "in New Zealand, they considered him the best full-back in the world".

Retiring after the 1995 World Cup, he had a spell in American Football with the Scottish Claymores before setting up a sports marketing agency. A talented golfer who brought the Ryder Cup to Scotland in 2014, he spends a lot of time raising awareness of Parkinson's, a disease that afflicts his wife of 29 years Diane.

PERCY MONTGOMERY

MAJOR TEAMS: Western Province, Stormers, Sharks, Dragons, Perpignan

Sometimes controversial but always mesmeric, Montgomery's rollercoaster Test career was a record-breaking one. He earned his first cap in 1997, five years after the Springboks returned to international action following the end of the apartheid, and with a blank canvas in terms of the history books, Montgomery set a series of South Africa milestones.

Unerringly accurate from the tee and blessed with devastating acceleration, his international bow came in the Springbok midfield in the second Test against the Lions in Durban. He scored a try on debut, crossing again in the third Test in Johannesburg, and by the end the 1997 Tri Nations, was already a fixture in the team.

Having won 50 caps, the full-back went into self-imposed international exile at the end of 2001 when he signed for Newport and relocated to Wales, but two years later South Africa relaxed its selection policy regarding overseas players. Montgomery was immediately recalled, top scoring in the 2004 Tri Nations as the Springboks were crowned southern hemisphere champions.

He was equally prolific as South Africa lifted the 2007 Rugby World Cup in France. The full-back accumulated 105 points in seven appearances, more than any other player, 12 of which came in the 15-6 victory over England in the final courtesy of four penalties from four attempts.

Further history beckoned in 2008 when he started against the All Blacks in Cape Town, becoming the first player ever to play 100 Tests for the Springboks. There were just two more international assignments and after coming off the bench in a 53-8 dismantling of the Wallabies, he called time on his South Africa career.

Position	Full-back
Country	South Africa
Test span	1997–2008
Test caps	102
Test points	893 (25T, 153C, 148P, 6DG)

He kicked two penalties against Australia to bring his overall haul to 893 points – 25 tries, 153 conversions, 148 penalties and six drop goals – in 102 games, and remains as the Springboks' all-time leading scorer.

KEN SCOTLAND

Game-changer Scotland altered full-back play forever

MAJOR TEAMS: Army, Heriot's FP, Cambridge University, London Scottish, Leicester, Aberdeenshire

In 1959 Ken Scotland took a ball on the run as part of a pre-planned Lions move and caught New Zealand completely off-guard. This wasn't meant to happen, but somehow this Scottish full-back was doing things differently. Very differently.

The tourists exposed the fallibility of the All Blacks that year despite losing the series 3-1, and the locals named Scotland as one of five standout players. He featured at fly-half, scrum-half and centre, but it was his play from full-back that caused the Kiwi writer TP McLean to remark, "He floated like summer down through the New Zealand defence."

Scotland changed full-back play forever. Gone were the rules, with the Scot prepared to attack from the back, picking lines rather than waiting to counter-attack; staging raids on enemy territory rather than hoofing the pill away. And he could kick off both feet too. He made place-kicking with the instep of the foot glamorous, when before it was considered ridiculous. An all-round athlete, he also received one cap for Scotland at cricket.

It's hard to fathom now, with his name lost amid a sea of greats, but the classier players of the age adored the effortless abandon of Scotland's play. At the time of his 50th Ireland cap, Tom Kiernan was asked who the finest player of his generation was. Instantly he replied, "Ken Scotland. It was a privilege to be on the same field as he was."

Position	Full-back
Country	Scotland
Test span	1957-65
Scotland caps	27 (27 starts)
Lions caps	5 (5 starts)
Test points	79 (8C, 16P, 5DG)

The playmaker was slight, even by past standards, and softly spoken. However, he was a dedicated tackler.

His Test career was cut short as he moved to North-East Scotland, but restrictions meant he couldn't play for the region's strongest FP clubs, so he had to join lowly, 'open' Aberdeenshire instead.

It may sound like his playing career faded, but Scotland inspired past greats and paved the way for the more adventurous 15s of the modern age. He retired as one of the game's finest innovators.

DON CLARKE

MAJOR TEAMS: Waikato

He wouldn't have troubled Christian Cullen, one of his Kiwi successors, in a foot race but class comes in different packages. And Don Clarke was class all right.

At 6ft 3in and over 17st, Clarke was a huge man for his era, and his powerful frame provided an intimidating sight for opponents. But his forte was his kicking – whether from hand or toe-kicking off the ground – and it's this aspect of his game that allows him to make our Top 10 at the expense of another great All Black, Bob Scott.

All told, Clarke scored 781 points in 89 games for New Zealand – a national record until surpassed by Grant Fox in 1988 – and a host of opponents had reason to curse his intervention with the boot. In 1959, the Lions scored four (three-point) tries to nil at Dunedin but lost to six Clarke penalties, while two years later in Wellington he landed an extraordinary kick to beat France; in an 80mph gale, he aimed the ball along the 25-yard line from wide out and watched the wind catch it and take it through the posts. "It was the most unbelievable kick I've ever seen," wrote the late Sir Terry McLean. His Test points include two goals from a mark, a scoring method long since outlawed. One of only two All Blacks to achieve a 'full house' in a Test, Clarke was one of five brothers to play for Waikato, and he was also a fine pace bowler, taking 117 first-class wickets for Northern Districts. Against the 1959 Lions he became the first All Black full-back to score a Test try – in New Zealand's 98th Test – and in eight years he was never dropped. He tasted defeat on just four occasions in 31 Tests.

Position	Full-back
Country	New Zealand
Test span	1956-64
Test caps	31 (31 starts)
Test points	207 (2T, 33C, 38P, 5DG, 2GfM)

Sir Wilson Whineray, Clarke's captain in all but six of his Tests, said, "He was like a huge energy force behind you and could have a devastating effect on the opposition."

Clarke emigrated to South Africa in the 1970s and set up a tree-felling business before passing away in 2002.

'The Boot' lines one up
Clarke was a prodigious kicker, from hand or off the floor

JPR WILLIAMS

MAJOR TEAMS: Bridgend, London Welsh, Natal, Tondu

It takes a special performer to become identifiable by three initials, but it was far more than the initials of JPR that canonised this formidable full-back into the legend of Welsh rugby. Flowing hair and prominent sideburns, allied to a full-blooded approach, made the Bridgend-born surgeon an unmistakable figure on the field of play.

An outstanding tennis player who won a junior competition at Wimbledon in 1966, Williams opted for rugby because its amateur status ensured he could continue with his medical studies.

He first gave notice of his talent on a 1968 development tour of Argentina, when he was dubbed 'Canasta' – Spanish for 'basket' – by home fans due to his unerring safety under the high ball. Having moved to St Mary's University and joined London Welsh, he was given a Test debut against Scotland in 1969 at the age of 19.

A maiden try arrived the next season,

White bait JPR scores against England

fittingly against England. On the way to representing Wales 55 times and collecting three Grand Slam titles, he would be on the winning side in all 11 of his Anglo-Welsh clashes.

Moments of astounding courage passed

Position	Full-back
Country	Wales
Test span	1969-81
Wales caps	55 (55 starts)
Lions caps	8 (8 starts)
Test points	39 (6T, 2C, 3P, 1DG)

into folklore. Given that Williams specialised in orthopaedics, bone-shuddering is an apt term to describe the hit that forced the French winger Jean-Francois Gourdon over the Cardiff Arms Park touchline in 1976.

More pivotal interventions came over eight Tests for the Lions. In 1974 Williams was a fundamental member of the 'Invincibles' outfit that saw off South Africa 3-0. Three years earlier his monster drop-goal in Auckland salvaged a 14-14 draw against New Zealand, securing the series 2-1.

He continued to play internationally into the 1980s, even starting one Test in Australia at flanker, and he was well into his fifties by the time he retired at Tondu in his hometown of Bridgend in 2003.

Coach Carwyn James poetically portrayed what Williams brought to his Lions team: "Like a forest animal he was blessed with the sixth sense for the presence of danger. It was an element he sought and loved. Fearless. Uncompromising. The competitor of competitors."

TOM KIERNAN

MAJOR TEAMS: Hawke's Bay, East Coast

Cool, calm, collected: Tom Kiernan never had a chance to escape greatness. The Irish Test selectors plucked him straight

Grey Fox The wily Kiernan excelled as a player and coach

from an Irish Universities side and from that moment on he was on a path strewn with broken records and trilling praise.

Barely into his twenties, Kiernan was picked to face the English in London and played with such assurance and swift thought that he won over a nation. He didn't have searing pace but had every other skill in his locker, scanning play from the back brilliantly and kicking goals with the best of them.

By the time he quit in 1973 he had every Irish record going: most caps (54), most points (158) and most games as captain (24).

As a Lion he twice toured South Africa. In 1962 he was in and out like a kitchen drawer thanks to injury, but in 1968 he was their bold captain – despite having initially declined to tour due to his job as an accountant. In the first Test he kicked 17 points and by the end he had scored 35 of the Lions' Test points – another record.

An accomplished covering defender, Kiernan had superb hands and could kick with either foot. The late Ray McLoughlin, who preceded him as Ireland captain, said he couldn't recall seeing him drop a ball.

Perhaps Kiernan's was a charmed life. He helped Ireland to their first win over South Africa with a mishit kick that crept over the bar, making it 9-6 in 1965. At the end of his reign, he led Ireland to a 10-10 draw with New Zealand in Dublin – Ireland's best result against the All Blacks until finally surpassed in 2016.

He also coached Munster to a 12-0 defeat of the All Blacks in Limerick, a match so famous they made a West End show about it. His playing days were done but Kiernan was still producing magic.

Position	Full-back
Country	Ireland
Test span	1960-73
Ireland caps	54 (54 starts)
Lions caps	5 (5 starts)
Test points	193 (2T, 27C, 42P, 2DG)

SERGE BLANCO

MAJOR TEAMS: Biarritz

The 1980s were the halcyon days of French rugby, where players wearing le coq would play with careless abandon, verve and a certain *je ne sais quoi*. Fitting the bill perfectly was Serge Blanco.

Born in Caracas to a Venezuelan mother, Blanco was nevertheless raised in the rugby hotbed of Biarritz, where, as a proud Basque, he stayed for his entire career, going on to become president of the club.

Blessed with the pace of a wing, ability to counter from anywhere on the field and a fiery temperament, Blanco was a dangerous adversary who went on to win 93 caps. Never the most vigorous of defenders, he routinely turned defence into attack, scoring 38 Test tries – still a French record 31 years after hanging up the boots.

After winning Grand Slams in 1981 and 1987, his most famous score came later that summer in the World Cup against Australia where he smoked (he did like his Gitanes) the covering Australian defence in the dying minutes of the semi-final to go over in the corner and put France into the final.

Position	Full-back
Country	France
Test span	1980-91
Test caps	93 (93 starts)
Test points	233 (38T, 6C, 21P, 2DG)

Another Blanco classic was as the catalyst for one of the greatest tries ever witnessed. With a typical cavalier attitude, he broke out from behind his try-line at Twickenham to spark a move that finished with Philippe Saint-André sprinting in beneath the posts 100m upfield.

Blanco's Test farewell, however, was a disappointment as France lost to England in the RWC 1991 quarter-finals with Blanco as captain.

Post-rugby, he has had a huge influence on French rugby as an administrator. He was a long-term president of the Ligue Nationale de Rugby (LNR) and was vice-president of the FFR from 2012-16. During that time he was called into Saint-André's coaching set-up as an unofficial adviser to help the misfiring French back-line. Commerce, too, has been kind to him, as the former mechanic now boasts a business empire that includes a clothing range and a luxury hotel chain.

Mercurial and enigmatic, Blanco had a presence that few could match.

Pelé du Rugby Blanco saw opportunities that others didn't and in 1991 he sparked one of the great tries v England

Wales centurion Halfpenny clocked up his 101st and final Test cap against the Barbarians in Cardiff in 2023

MAJOR TEAMS: Neath, Cardiff RFC, Cardiff Blues, Toulon, Scarlets, Crusaders, Harlequins

One of only nine players to have registered the fabled century of caps for Wales, Halfpenny's international career spanned 15 years, three Lions tours, and most notably a series of standout individual displays for the Principality as Warren Gatland's side claimed the Six Nations Grand Slam in 2012.

First capped on the wing as a 19-year-old against South Africa in Cardiff in the autumn of 2008, he quickly established himself as his

LEIGH HALFPENNY

country's first-choice full-back. In 2012 his signature accuracy with the boot propelled Wales to their first Championship clean sweep for four years, with Halfpenny's personal haul of 66 points earning him the accolades as the tournament's top scorer that year. He was voted the Six Nations Player of the Tournament in 2017.

A rock in defence despite his stature, Halfpenny was the youngest of the 37 players selected for the 2009 Lions tour to South Africa. The 2013 trip to Australia, however, was the pinnacle of his career for the famous tourists, starting all three Tests in a 2-1 series triumph and winning the coveted Player of the Series award. The 49 points from his trusty right boot Down Under broke the previous series record set by compatriot Stephen Jones in South Africa four years earlier. He travelled with the Lions for a third time in 2017, featuring as a substitute in the first Test against the All Blacks in Auckland.

His 101st and final game for his country came in 2023 in the World Cup against Portugal in Nice. He retired from Wales duty with a record of 801 points in red, behind only Neil Jenkins (1,049) and Jones (917) on the list of the Principality's leading scorers.

At club level Halfpenny has represented Neath, Cardiff, Blues, Toulon, Scarlets, Crusaders and most recently Harlequins. He won the European Champions Cup with Toulon in 2015, kicking 14 points in the final against Clermont Auvergne. He was also an Anglo-Welsh Cup champion in 2009 with Cardiff, scoring two tries against Gloucester in a 50-12 demolition at Twickenham, and a European Challenge Cup winner the following season.

Position	Full-back
Country	Wales
Test span	2008–2023
Test caps	101
Lions caps	4
Test points	801 (15T, 81C, 187P, 1DG)

ANDY IRVINE

MAJOR TEAMS: Heriot's

The owner of an extremely accurate right boot from the kicking tee, Andy Irvine holds two British & Irish Lions scoring records that may remain unassailable for a while yet.

The first is the amount of points on a tour of South Africa: 156 in 15 matches in 1974. The achievement is all the more remarkable considering that JPR Williams's presence restricted him to just two Test appearances on the wing.

Irvine's second Lions best comes from his cumulative total of 274 in 42 appearances, supplemented by more success in New Zealand in 1977 – including five tries as Kings Country-Wanganui were beaten 60-9 – and back in South Africa as an injury replacement in 1980.

However, to pigeonhole him as merely a sharpshooter would be to overlook his exciting, incisive running from full-back. Blistering pace and a wicked step off either foot could slice opposition defences apart and he often provided thrilling counter-punches from backfield.

Winning 51 caps for Scotland between 1972 and 1982, he earned induction into the World Rugby Hall of Fame in 1999.

Commentary doyen Bill McLaren had a soft spot for the Edinburgh-born veteran of Heriot's, putting him on a par with Australian David Campese as one of the sport's great entertainers.

"Both men were adventurers," he said. "When they got the ball, they were prepared to tilt the lance. Sometimes it didn't come off but most of the time it did. They lit up matches with their brilliance and because of that they made commentary a piece of toffee."

And Scotland legend Jim Telfer calls Irvine the best attacking player he has ever seen. "His pace and power cut defences to pieces and he often won games single-handedly, such was his presence. He was also a very good captain."

Following his retirement, Irvine coached Heriot's before being appointed Scottish Rugby Union president in 2005. Two years later he joined the Lions committee as chairman and became team manager for the 2013 tour of Australia.

Position	Full-back
Country	Scotland
Test span	1972-82
Scotland caps	51 (51 starts)
Lions caps	9 (9 starts)
Test points	301 (12T, 26C, 67P)

Fun of the flair Irvine was captivating to watch

CHRISTIAN CULLEN

Bullet train Cullen glides past Tonga at the 1999 World Cup

MAJOR TEAMS: Manawatu, Wellington, Hurricanes, Munster

Like a lightning bolt, Christian Cullen flashed dramatically into the rugby firmament and then disappeared, his Test career ending when he was only 26.

It was time enough to imprint himself on the game as arguably the best attacking full-back in history, and only Doug Howlett (49) has scored more Test tries than Cullen (46) for the All Blacks.

Growing up in Paekakariki, north of Wellington, Cullen was a big fish in a small pond at Kapiti College, making his first XV debut at 15 and becoming a goalkicking centre. In 1996, at the age of 20, he burst into the nation's consciousness with his Man of the Tournament showing at the Hong Kong Sevens. He set records for the most tries (18) and points (136), and coach Gordon Tietjens called it the greatest sevens performance he had seen.

Cullen's career exploded. On his Test debut against Samoa he was cut in half by a Brian Lima tackle but bounced up to score a hat-trick. In his next game, against Scotland, he beat seven defenders for the first of his four tries. "Lomu is the devil we know," said Scotland captain Rob Wainwright, "Cullen is the one we're learning about."

Cullen's gliding running style, with no pumping of the arms and no obvious exertion, was one of the great sights in the game. Although he could step off both feet, he frequently beat players by deception, and his timing into the line was exceptional.

The man dubbed the 'Paekakariki Express' became a try-scoring machine, and by the time he faced France in 2000 he had become the fifth man to play 50 consecutive Tests, after McBride, Edwards, Fitzpatrick and Roff. That run included a few caps at wing and, at the 1999 World Cup, at outside-centre.

In 2001 Cullen fell out of favour with new ABs coach John Mitchell, so he upped sticks to Munster, where his career fizzled out in 2007 after a series of injuries.

Position	Full-back
Country	New Zealand
Test span	1996-2002
Test caps	58 (56 starts)
Test points	236 (46T, 3C)

RUGBY LEGENDS

WINGS

First and foremost, wings should run like the wind – though the ability to accelerate quickly is more meaningful than a player's time over 100m. Beating a defender through feints, shimmies and sidesteps is desirable, and if you also carry 16st-plus of ballast into contact then so much the better. Defensively, wings must be utterly fearless and dependable under the high ball and have the tactical awareness to cover the backfield, working in a pendulum with your fellow wing and full-back. Above all, wings must be deadly finishers and must relish the limelight – you can be very exposed out there!

SNCF

TONY O'REILLY

MAJOR TEAMS: Old Belvedere, Leicester Tigers, London Irish

When you evaluate Tony O'Reilly's rugby career, it's hard to look beyond the scoring records. The flame-haired wing is still the Lions' top try-scorer with 38 in 38 appearances, as well as the Barbarians' top try-scorer with 30 in 38 run-outs. O'Reilly also did longevity, with the longest Five Nations career of 15 years and 23 days, a record he shared with Mike Gibson until overtaken by Italy's Mauro Bergamasco.

Souvenir O'Reilly arrives home from the 1959 Lions tour

The Dubliner made his debut for Ireland at 18 against France, when straight out of Belvedere College, and took his final bow against England at 33, thus depriving Frank O'Driscoll (father of Brian) of his chance of a cherished cap.

His final cap, as a late call-up due to an injury, ended a seven-year Test hiatus and he did well to last the game at Twickenham as he was strictly a social player by then at London Irish. He spent most of the match in a daze after a blow to the head.

Tall for a wing at 6ft 2in, and nearly 15st, O'Reilly was swift over the ground, a fine reader of the game and a brilliant finisher. He reserved his greatest feats for the Lions, for whom he felt more of an affinity in terms of style. "I loved the freedom that I didn't get with Ireland, the thrill of receiving the ball ten or 15 times in a game. The Lions played running rugby and I was a runner."

He first toured with the 1955 Lions to South Africa as a teenager, where he scored 16 tries in 15 games, including the key score in the 23-22 first-Test win in Johannesburg.

He was even more prolific four years later in Australia and New Zealand, scoring 22 tries – four of them in the Tests.

Amusingly, O'Reilly's physique might have helped make him a film star, after a casting director invited him for a meeting with the director of *Ben Hur*. O'Reilly didn't turn up and Charlton Heston eventually won an Oscar playing the lead role.

When O'Reilly hung up his boots, as a natural networker with a quick wit, it was no surprise to see him going on to enjoy a stellar journey in business and philanthropy. He became chairman of food processing giant HJ Heinz and regularly adorned *The Sunday Times Rich List*.

In recent years he encountered financial trouble and had to sell some assets.

Position	Wing
Country	Ireland
Test span	1955-70
Ireland caps	29 (29 starts)
Lions caps	10 (10 starts)
Test points	30 (10T)

RORY UNDERWOOD

MAJOR TEAMS: Leicester, Bedford Blues

More than 25 years after his final Test for England, Rory Underwood is still the nation's record try-scorer. That says all you need to know about the class of this outstandingly talented wing, especially as the nearest challenger to his tally of 50, Jonny May, is still in the thirties.

Born in Middlesbrough in 1963 to a Chinese-Malaysian mother and English father, Underwood was educated at Barnard Castle. He spent most of his playing days at Leicester Tigers, scoring 134 tries in 236 appearances, before ending his career at Bedford, where he scored 12 tries in 23 Premiership matches in the 1998-99 season – at the age of 35.

His pace was renowned but many overlook the strength he brought to bear in contact. When England first started to take conditioning seriously in the late 1980s, one of

the tests involved throwing a 16lb shot two-handed over your head. To everyone's surprise, Underwood threw it furthest. "Pound for pound, he was the most powerful athlete we had," said Don Rutherford, the RFU's then technical director.

It enabled him to brush off tacklers, yet former England team-mate Brian Moore believes Underwood could have been even more lethal if he had taken nutrition seriously. Moore says the winger had "the most astonishingly bad diet you could imagine for such an outstanding athlete... chips, Coke, pizzas, burgers, ice cream, sweets. He was like a kid and was the first to admit it". Even so, Underwood helped England win three Grand Slams and a Five Nations title in the 1990s, as well as playing in six Lions Tests. From 1992 he had the pleasure of playing on the opposite wing to his younger brother Tony with England.

Away from rugby, Underwood was an RAF pilot for 18 years and a long-time director at the Tigers. Awarded an MBE in 1995, he runs a management business, Wingman Performance Consultants. His lives in Lincolnshire with his wife.

Position	Wing
Country	England
Test span	1984-96
England caps	85 (85 starts)
Lions caps	7 (7 starts)
Test points	215 (50T)

RUPENI CAUCAUNIBUCA

Titan of Toulouse Caucau has a lie-down during a Top 14 match in 2011

MAJOR TEAMS: Northland, Auckland Blues, Agen, Toulouse

If you were to design a rugby player for the YouTube generation, your prototype would look like Rupeni Caucaunibuca. Known universally as 'Caucau', the Fijian wing ranks second only to Jonah Lomu for his ability to astound on the pitch.

After starting out in sevens, Caucau first came to the attention of global audiences at the 2003 World Cup with Fiji, although not before he had shunned All Black advances after a scintillating season with the Blues. First, there was a sensational 60m individual try against France, followed swiftly by a yellow card for fighting – a sign of things to come.

Next, against Scotland, he scored within two minutes with an audacious finish in the corner. His second try was even more outrageous as he skipped and sidestepped past flailing Scots defenders from Fiji's 22, leading the commentator to exclaim, "Give it to Caucau and he is go-go, gone!" A shell-shocked Chris Paterson said, "He can be the world's best player, the type who can win a game almost on his own."

After the World Cup the chequebooks were out for his signature. He plumped for Agen in the Top 14, where he stayed for five helter-skelter years, scoring 65 tries. In this period, his Test appearances were fleeting, though his scoring ratio never diminished.

Position	Wing
Country	Fiji
Test span	2003-10
Fiji caps	7 (7 starts)
Pacific Islanders caps	1 (1 start)
Test points	50 (10T)

Caucau was almost as famous for his off-field indiscipline as his on-field play. Stories would drift over the Channel that Caucau had gone missing back in Fiji and was infuriating coaches, but, more often than not, he'd return with a big smile, turn in a match-winning performance and be forgiven.

Similarly, he would frustrate national coaches, and his charge sheet included a one-year ban for missing training camps and a three-month ban for testing positive for cannabis use.

After a spell at Toulouse, during which he propelled them into the Top 14 final with a semi-final brace against Clermont, he returned to Agen before leaving France in 2014. Today he lives back in Fiji and in the recent documentary *Oceans Apart*, he said he was bankrupt having spent all his money on drinking and handouts.

BRYAN HABANA

Menace of Saint-Denis Habana scores in the RWC 2007 semi-final against Argentina in Paris

MAJOR TEAMS: Golden Lions, Blue Bulls, Bulls, Stormers, Toulon

Bryan Gary Habana was named after two footballers – Bryan Robson and Gary Bailey of Man Utd fame – but spent 15 years terrorising elite rugby defences rather than soccer ones. He chalked up records quicker than he sprinted past opponents, scoring ten tries in his first ten Tests and 15 in his first 20 before becoming the first South African to touch down 50 times in Test rugby when crossing Samoa's line in 2013.

We should have seen this torrent of tries coming after Habana, who was inspired by seeing the Boks win the 1995 World Cup, top-scored in the U21 World Championship in 2004 and made his Test debut the same year.

Coming off the bench against England at Twickenham, Habana scored with his first touch and hardly stopped thereafter, whether playing for South Africa, the Bulls, the Stormers or Toulon in France. Eight tries at RWC 2007 helped see him crowned as World Rugby Player of the Year. Earlier that year he had scored the winning try in the Super 14 Final for the Bulls against the Sharks in stoppage time. After his four-try World Cup haul in a 59-7 victory over Samoa, Springboks coach Jake White beamed, "The way he went outside, inside, underneath those people was amazing."

A master of the intercept, Habana assembled one of the biggest collections of winner's medals in the game. On top of the

Position	Wing
Country	South Africa
Test span	2004-16
Test caps	124 (122 starts)
Test points	335 (67T)

2007 World Cup, he won two Super Rugby titles, a Tri-Nations, two European Cups and a French Top 14 title and he became the fourth South African to reach a century of caps – after Percy Montgomery, John Smit and Victor Matfield – in 2014. Only Matfield (127) lies ahead of him on the Boks' caps list, while Habana's 67 Test tries is bettered only by Japan's Daisuke Ohata (69).

In 2007 Habana, who clocked 10.2 seconds for 100m, raced a cheetah as part of a conservation campaign. For once he finished as a runner-up.

DAVID CAMPESE

MAJOR TEAMS: ACT, Padova, Randwick, New South Wales, Milan

The son of a wine-making Italian immigrant, Australian David Campese has managed to upset almost everyone because of his truculence and outspoken views. The game is no worse for that.

His distaste for modern 'bash and recycle' rugby is unsurprising when you consider the running skills and devil-may-care attitude with which he burnished the Test stage 101 times. It occasionally left him with egg on his face, but 64 tries – placing him third in the all-time list – tells its own story.

At his best he was utterly unstoppable, his weaving in-out runs and mesmerising footwork illuminating the final decade of amateurism. He was a mean kicker of a ball too, but above all it was his desire to attack from all areas that scared opponents witless.

Brought up on league in ACT, Campese switched codes and burst into global consciousness during the 1984 European tour that yielded a Wallaby Grand Slam.

By RWC 1991 he was at the peak of his powers and two celebrated runs – one arrow-straight, the other mischievously mazy – accounted for the All Blacks on the way to lifting the trophy at Twickenham.

The onus on increased physical power, as rugby careered towards professionalism, worked against Campese, who was heavier (by 10kg) and slower by RWC 1995.

In October 1996 he became only the second Test centurion – behind Philippe Sella – when facing Italy in Padua, close to where his father was born. The same year he nearly accepted an offer to join Saracens.

He is officially deemed rugby union's 71st professional player. Yet the tag makes him smile because, long before rugby went open, he played for many years in Italy during off-seasons – and he was certainly well rewarded for his trouble.

Position	Wing
Country	Australia
Test span	1982-96
Test caps	101 (100 starts)
Test points	315 (64T, 8C, 7P, 2DG)

Untouchable Campese leaves the Welsh defence for dead during a 38-3 RWC 1991 victory for the Wallabies

JASON ROBINSON

MAJOR TEAMS: Wigan RL, Bath, Sale

When Clive Woodward helped bring league star Jason Robinson to union at the turn of the century, he was signing far more than a deadly finisher with a jagged step that could stump a defender within a stride.

The 5ft 8in Yorkshireman brought incredible professionalism to an England camp not long out of the amateur era, with Jonny Wilkinson saying Robinson's arrival forced him to re-evaluate his game. "His ability to beat players both ways, and make 90-degree direction changes without losing speed, obliterated what I believed were the limits for footwork and speed."

Robinson went on to master union as he had league, becoming a world champion in 2003 after scoring England's only try of the final against the Wallabies and punching the ball in celebration high into the Sydney stands.

Two years earlier, he had made the Lions Test team in the same country having not yet started for England. After scoring five tries on his Lions debut in a provincial fixture, Robinson bamboozled Chris Latham in the proverbial telephone box to set the tourists on their way to victory in Brisbane. Coach Graham Henry hailed him as "a Gerald Davies for the new millennium".

Ironically, Robinson started more games at full-back (28) than wing (19) for England, and those who doubted his ability to catch the high ball were soon assuaged by his athletic prowess – he had a 3ft standing jump that enabled him to outleap far taller men.

Robinson was to captain England before he wound things up at the 2007 World Cup final, playing through the pain having damaged a hamstring in the warm-up.

Thus ended a career that included an English title with Sale, seven England and 12 GB caps in league, and 171 tries in 273 starts for Wigan. He went on to coach Sale and had a brief playing stint at Fylde before finally calling time for good in July 2011.

A born-again Christian who called a halt to the heavy drinking that scarred his early years as a pro sportsman, Robinson is sixth on the all-time England try list with 28.

Position	Wing
Country	England
Test span	2001-07
England caps	51 (47 starts)
Lions caps	5 (5 starts)
Test points	150 (30T)

Scorcher Scoring against Australia in the RWC 2003 final

GERALD DAVIES

MAJOR TEAMS: Llanelli, Cambridge University, London Welsh, Cardiff

Such was Davies's fame during the late 1960s and 1970s that he was known by a single name: Gerald. With jet-black locks, a heavy moustache and a jackhammer sidestep, Davies was a debonair figure who in a split-second could thrust himself through the tightest of midfield gaps.

He was also an instinctive finisher, often leaping like a salmon to dot down inside the corner flag with millimetres to spare. One of his more devastating performances came in a cup tie for Cardiff against Pontypool when, despite seeing little ball, he managed to score four tries.

A star turn for Cardiff and London Welsh between 1965 and 1974, it was on the international stage that Davies made his name. Early in his Wales career he played as a centre until coach Clive Rowlands encouraged him to move to the wing in 1969, where he played with such poise until his final game.

Davies played in three Grand Slam campaigns, 1971, 1976 and 1978 – one of a handful of Welsh players to achieve this feat. John Dawes, his captain on the 1971 Lions tour, said, "He was a magical man to have in your team because he could turn a game with one run. Some of the tries he scored were breathtaking."

Davies was one of many who further enhanced his reputation with the British & Irish Lions, touring against the Springboks in 1968 and the All Blacks in 1971, where he crossed the whitewash on three occasions and helped the Lions to their only Test-series win in New Zealand to date.

An academic scholar who spent three years at Cambridge reading English, Davies refused to tour South Africa in 1974 in protest at apartheid.

It came as no surprise that in his retirement he pursued a successful career in journalism with *The Times* and latterly sports administration with the Welsh Rugby Union and the Lions. He's currently president of the WRU, an office he will hold until the end of next year's World Cup.

Welsh wizard Davies had a magical step

Position	Wing
Country	Wales
Test span	1966-78
Wales caps	46 (46 starts)
Lions caps	5 (5 starts)
Test points	81 (23T)

JOHN KIRWAN

MAJOR TEAMS: Auckland, Treviso, Auckland Warriors, NEC Green Rockets

Position	Wing
Country	New Zealand
Test span	1984-94
Test caps	63 (62 starts)
Test points	143 (35T)

When John Kirwan sprinted and swerved from his own 22 to cross the Italy try-line during the very first World Cup match in 1987, the All Black couldn't have guessed that try would still be rated by many as the greatest scored at a RWC tournament fully 35 years later. But it was just one example of the unstoppable attacking force that was Kirwan, as he shredded defences like paper throughout his career.

He scored six tries at that World Cup, including two in the semi-final win over Wales and one in the final against France (and two days later was back chopping meat in his dad's butcher's shop). The next year Kirwan was at it again, notching ten tries in a five-Test salvo, including four against Wales in Christchurch – he ended his All Blacks career with a 79% win rate.

What made him so deadly? He was quick, powerful and had a swerve that could wrong-foot oncoming defenders, and he stood 6ft 4in, which was huge for a wing in that era. After the 1987 World Cup semi-final he gave Mark Ring his shorts as a memento, and when Ring gave them to Wales lock Huw Richards to try on, there was a problem. "Their wing's shorts were too big for our second-row: enough said," wrote Ring in his autobiography, *Ring Master*.

Kirwan came from Marist Brothers Old Boys into the Auckland side in 1983 when he was 18 and within a year he was making his Test debut. He won the Ranfurly Shield and NPC with Auckland and scored an astonishing eight tries in one match against North Otago in 1993.

Other teams to benefit from Kirwan's talents were Treviso in Italy, the Auckland Warriors rugby league side from 1995-96, and NEC Green Rockets in Japan, his last club before retiring in 1999.

He went on to coach two national teams, Italy from 2002-05 and Japan from 2007-11, as well as the Blues from 2013-15.

Kirwan was knighted for services to mental health awareness and rugby after writing about suffering from depression in his book *All Blacks Don't Cry*.

Punch and panache Kirwan shredded defences like paper

SHANE WILLIAMS

MAJOR TEAMS: Neath, Ospreys, Mitsubishi Dynaboars

Shane Williams was watching as a replacement scrum-half when injuries left his Neath team short of a wing during a 1998 cup tie against Wrexham. Would Shane be happy to fill in?

Of course he would, and so was born the career of one of the all-time great finishers, with Williams going on to score 60 Test tries – one of only four men to ever reach that lofty landmark.

Williams's origins as a scrawny working-class kid from the Amman Valley, so shy that on his Wales debut he pretended not to hear when he was summoned from the bench, make his rise all the more romantic. At 5ft 7in tall and 11st soaking wet, he was forced to defy critics who felt he would be tossed about like a rag doll on the international stage.

Largely ignored under Graham Henry, Williams tried bulking up but sustained a series of torn hamstrings and muscle strains as he reached an unnatural size and weight.

So he changed tack and in 2003, having been taken to the World Cup initially as a third-choice No 9, he was unleashed on the wing against the All Blacks. Williams had spent the week quarantined with a sick bug but he was on fire that night in Sydney, his quick feet and magical sidestep tormenting the Kiwis.

Position	Wing
Country	Wales
Test span	2000-11
Wales caps	87 (84 starts)
Lions caps	4 (3 starts)
Test points	300 (60T)

Williams was rarely overlooked again. In 2008, after scoring 14 tries in 11 Tests and famously taunting South Africa's Bryan Habana by shouting "Mismatch!" at his opposite number, he was named World Rugby's Player of the Year.

He played in two Lions series, bagging two tries against the Springboks in 2009, but more significant than his try-scoring were the thrilling skills and brio he brought to the game. He credits much of his balance and explosiveness on the field to his passion for gymnastics as a youngster.

Typically, he went out with a splash by scoring in the final play of his final Test, against Australia in 2011.

Arm's length Williams hands off Wallaby Berrick Barnes during RWC 2011

JONAH LOMU

Wrecking ball Lomu on his way to a four-try haul against England at RWC 1995

MAJOR TEAMS: Counties Manukau, Wellington, Auckland

This summer will mark the 27th anniversary of Jonah Lomu becoming rugby's first bona fide global superstar. A teenager when the tournament started, Lomu's name can legitimately be linked with the term 'shock and awe' at the 1995 World Cup.

Growing up in South Auckland, he started out playing rugby league but at the age of 14 switched to union with Wesley College. A superb schoolboy athlete, he was clocked at 10.8 seconds over 100m.

This speed, allied to his 6ft 5in, 19st frame, meant his impact on the game was profound, with jumbo-sized imitators like George North, Alesana Tuilagi and Julian Savea all boasting elements of his game.

In 1995, Lomu, who had made his New Zealand debut at the Hong Kong Sevens the previous year, scored three tries against Ireland and Scotland. But it was when he faced Will Carling's England that his star went stratospheric – his performance was so remarkable that it set rugby on the path towards professionalism, with television channels prepared to pay serious money for athletes of Lomu's calibre.

He scored four tries against England but it was the first, when he swatted Tony Underwood away and trampled over Mike Catt, that left fans and opponents dumbstruck. Though he was shackled in the final, Lomu's celebrity soon saw a Sony PlayStation game named after him.

Position	Wing
Country	New Zealand
Test span	1994-2002
Test caps	63 (54 starts)
Test points	185 (37T)

At the 1999 World Cup, Lomu lived up to his reputation, scoring eight tries. One image that encapsulated his power came against France in the semi-final when full-back Xavier Garbajosa simply skipped out of the way as Lomu careered towards him on his way to the line. "He was like a tower block running at you," Jason Robinson once said.

Lomu was to play his final Test for New Zealand in 2002 at just 27, when a debilitating kidney complaint started to affect his ability to perform at the highest level. He took his leave with 37 tries.

In 2015, Lomu died from a heart attack at the age of just 40. He remains unsurpassed as a rugby icon, with many of today's stars citing him as their greatest inspiration.

RUGBY LEGENDS

CENTRES

The inside-centre (12) and outside-centre (13) work in unison, but don't think of them as two peas from the same pod. Between them they encompass many different qualities, and an outstanding 12 could be ineffective at 13, and vice versa. The 12 might be a bludgeon who crashes the ball up, or equally they might act as a 'second fly-half', with kicking skills and immaculate passing distribution. At 13, you must have more pace, preferably the sort to take you arcing round your marker to create a two-on-one, and both players should be defensively impeccable.

JEAN DE VILLIERS

MAJOR TEAMS: Western Province, Stormers, Munster, Leicester Tigers

The perfect blend of power of power and poise, De Villiers' early international forays came on the wing, but it was in the heart of the South Africa midfield that he forged his reputation. Of his 109 Tests for his country, 94 came at 12 to make the Stormers legend the most capped centre in Springbok history.

He made his international debut at the age of 21 against France in 2002 and after recovering from a major knee injury, was a standout performer for the Boks in the 2004 Tri-Nations. De Villiers was the competition's joint top try scorer with three, including a score in the 40-26 demolition of the All Blacks in Johannesburg, as Jake White's team claimed the title.

Selected for the victorious South Africa squad for the 2007 Rugby World Cup in France, De Villiers started the opening group stage clash with Samoa in Paris, but his

involvement in the tournament lasted just 43 minutes after he suffered a torn bicep.

A player who opted for the direct approach in attack and defence, 2009 was his greatest year of international rugby as the Springboks defeated the Lions and were then crowned the champions of the southern hemisphere. He started the triumphant first and second Tests against the Lions in Durban and Pretoria and played all six games in the subsequent successful Tri-Nations campaign.

In the summer of 2012 he was named South Africa captain for the two-Test series against England. In total, he led his country 37 times, a record only surpassed by John Smit and Siya Kilosi. Two years later he became the fifth player to win a century of Springbok caps when he lined up against New Zealand in Wellington. He announced his international retirement after the 2015 Rugby World Cup in England.

A veteran of more than 100 games for the Stormers, he twice ventured north to play club rugby in Europe, representing Munster and Leicester before finally hanging up his boots in 2016.

Position	Centre
Country	South Africa
Test span	2002–15
Test caps	109
Test points	135 (27T)

PHILIPPE SELLA

Midas touch Sella had all the skills

MAJOR TEAMS: Agen

For becoming the first player to win 100 Test caps, Philippe Sella is guaranteed a place in rugby's hall of fame. The gallery of leading French threequarters is adorned by the portraits of artists who were touched by genius, but when he retired as the game's most-capped player with 111 caps to his name, he was universally appreciated as one of rugby's old masters.

Sella had entered the French side in 1982, playing on the wing after gaining the unusual distinction of school, youth and student honours.

As a stripling with a zest for total rugby, he was a fast and elusive runner. But the natural toughness and easy fitness that went with his rural Garonne upbringing perfectly equipped him for a role at centre, a position he quickly made his own.

The quality that marked Sella out among the panoply of brilliant French backs was the range of his skills. His flair for attacking rugby placed him on the same pedestal as the Boniface brothers, Jo Maso, Didier Codorniou and Denis Charvet.

But the extra dimension to his game that his illustrious predecessors lacked was stoical defence. Sella relished making a clattering tackle as much as scoring any of his 30 Test tries – tries that included one in each Five Nations game in 1986, when he became only the fourth man in history to perform the feat, and a lung-bursting 65m run at Twickenham in 1987 off a delicious interception that bore all the hallmarks of his class.

When Sella retired after the 1995 World Cup in South Africa, he left a huge vacuum in les Bleus' back-line – one that, arguably, they have never quite managed to fill.

Position	Centre
Country	France
Test span	1982-95
Test caps	111 (110 starts)
Test points	125 (30T)

JEREMY GUSCOTT

Catch me if you can The whippet-like Guscott took some stopping in full flight

MAJOR TEAMS: Bath

The grander the stage, the greater the response – that's what Lions legend Sir Ian McGeechan calls the hallmark of a "Test-match animal". And in Jeremy Guscott, the elegant Englishman whose gliding running graced Test rugby for a decade, he found just such a player.

The Bathonian took centre stage for the Lions not once but twice, making crucial interventions to steer the tourists to series success eight years apart. His first act, against the 1989 Wallabies, came in only his second Test after he had become the first England debutant to score a hat-trick since Dan Lambert against France in 1907.

That feat, in Romania, set McGeechan's antenna twitching, and when Will Carling withdrew from the Lions tour with shin splints, he thrust the 24-year-old apprentice bricklayer into his Lions squad. Guscott rewarded his faith with a glorious winning try to turn the series, stabbing a grubber kick behind the Aussie midfield, stepping on the accelerator and gathering the beneficent bounce to score under the posts. "It was a mega moment," he said.

It was the first of many as Guscott established himself alongside Carling in a titanic England midfield partnership. Guscott's blistering acceleration enabled him to track runners and exploit line breaks – when he wasn't making them himself. He racked up the scores for club and country and might have been even more prolific had he been paired with his kindred spirit at Bath, the fly-half Stuart Barnes. They played together for England on just two occasions.

Guscott's effortless pace also helped make him a marvellous defender, as he showed on the 1993 Lions tour in New Zealand.

Three Grand Slams and fifth place on England's all-time try list with 30 would give him superstar status even without his Lions heroics, which reached new heights with his drop-goal in Durban to beat the 1997 Springboks. It was an instinctive moment of magic from a player who always kicked beautifully, having been a fly-half until 19.

Guscott retired after a groin injury suffered at RWC 1999. After being a bus driver, model and PR man as well as a bricklayer, he worked for the BBC for more than 20 years until February 2022.

Position	Centre
Country	England
Test span	1989–99
England caps	65 (62 starts)
Lions caps	8 (8 starts)
Test points	150 (31T, 3DG)

YANNICK JAUZION

MAJOR TEAMS: Colomiers, Toulouse

The professional era has seen midfields crowded with mighty collisions between hulking figures on a quest to cross the all-important gain-line. Standing just shy of 6ft 4in and weighing around 17st, Yannick Jauzion didn't want for size. Even so, he stood out from the crowd as a centre who combined impressive power and athleticism with easy, elegant skills.

Jauzion traded Colomiers for neighbours Toulouse in 2002, a year after making his debut for France in a thrilling 32-23 win over South Africa at Ellis Park. He would become a totem wearing black and red under Guy Novès, inspiring Le Stade to three Top 14 titles as well as a trio of Heineken Cup crowns.

A master of the offload who also hit incisive running lines, Jauzion was the unfussy facilitator around which a team could mould their attacking approach.

Indeed, although a 73-Test France career yielded 20 tries, his smooth distribution and ability to free his arms in the contact area to find onrushing team-mates were more significant attributes. Grand Slams in 2002, 2004 and 2010 came either side of another Six Nations championship triumph in 2007, the same year that Jauzion scored to oust the All Blacks in the World Cup quarter-finals and earned a World Rugby Player of the Year nomination.

Pioneering English backs coach Brian Ashton labelled Toulouse's fluent best as "absolutely phenomenal" and "on a totally different level to what anyone else plays, even the All Blacks". Whether at 12 or 13, Jauzion was the lynchpin to this irresistible style. Teams needed to develop innovative plans – as Wasps did by positioning back-rower Joe Worsley in the back-line from lineouts – in order to quell his influence.

Like Ashton, *Rugby World*'s Stuart Barnes is another man who doesn't need any convincing of the centre's supreme talents. "The Jauzion offload looks easy," said the former England fly-half, "but only those verging on greatness make sport seem so simple."

Centre parting Jauzion was the world's best midfielder at RWC 2007

Position	Centre
Country	France
Test span	2001-11
Test caps	73 (65 starts)
Test points	103 (20T, 1DG)

MIKE GIBSON

MAJOR TEAMS: North of Ireland, Cambridge University

New Zealanders regarded Belfast-born Mike Gibson as the most complete midfield player of a generation. He filled the lead role for Ireland and the Lions in one of the game's longest-running shows, his representative act embracing a then-world record 69 caps and a dozen Lions Tests between 1964 and 1979.

Gibson's vision and reading of the game was first revealed while playing at outside-half. He was an elusive runner who used a convincing dummy to unlock defences for Cambridge in the 1963 Varsity Match and was fast-tracked into Ireland's side for the Five Nations.

On his debut he spurred them to a convincing 18-5 win against England at Twickenham, where his uncanny instinct to anticipate complex moves several phases ahead led critics to describe him as rugby's equivalent of a chess grandmaster.

Ulster roar Gibson went on five Lions tours

It was this remarkable perception that made Gibson as dangerous a player in defence as he was in attack. Everything about his game bore the hallmark of genius. His speed off the mark and sparkling sidestep proved just as valuable as his off-the-ball running when covering threatening situations.

Later in his career Gibson the centre was even better than Gibson the out-half, because the new position offered him greater scope to choose his options.

His finest hours were with the British & Irish Lions, with whom he made a record five tours. In New Zealand in 1966 he was the standout player in a modest side, playing centre to accommodate Dai Watkins at fly-half in the Test series.

But his biggest contribution came in 1971 when, for the only time to date, the Lions took a rubber off the All Blacks. He starred at centre outside Barry John throughout that series, and his performances particularly impressed Colin Meads, the New Zealand talisman, who paid the Irishman the highest compliment by saying, "Gibson's presence in the Lions back-line was the most frustrating influence of all.

Position	Centre
Country	Ireland
Test span	1964-79
Ireland caps	69 (69 starts)
Lions caps	12 (11 starts)
Test points	112 (9T, 7C, 16P, 6DG)

WILL GREENWOOD

MAJOR TEAMS: Harlequins, Leicester Tigers

One of a rare group of players to tour with the Lions before he had represented his country, Greenwood was selected for the 1997 series against South Africa. He made his England bow in a 15-15 draw against the Wallabies at Twickenham later the same year and in 2003 later was a mainstay for the Red Rose in their famous World Cup triumph Down Under.

A tall but relatively slight inside centre, the son of former England coach Dick Greenwood inside forged a reputation as a talented midfield playmaker in the Clive Woodward era as his team dominated the early years of the recently expanded Six Nations. Greenwood featured in both the 2000 and 2001 campaigns as the Red Rose were crowned champions and was an ever-present in 2003 when the Grand Slam was secured.

His undisputed career highlight came with World Cup glory in Australia. Playing in three of the four group games, he was

the only try scorer in white in the 28-17 quarter-final defeat of Wales and on the pitch for every dramatic minute of normal and extra-time in the final in Sydney as England emerged 20-17 winners over their hosts. He remains a member of an exclusive club of players from the northern hemisphere to have broken their southern counterpart's ongoing stranglehold on the silverware.

Injury ruled him out of contention for the Tests on the 1997 Lions tour against the Springboks but he belatedly won his first full cap for the tourists eight years later in New Zealand, featuring from the bench in the first game of the series against the All Blacks in Christchurch before starting the third and final match at Eden Park.

Despite his reputation as a deft, creative force, he was also a prolific finisher. He scored 31 tries in only 55 appearances for his country, leaving him joint third on the Red Rose's all-time list, eclipsing fellow centre Jeremy Guscott's haul of 30 in 65 Tests. His England career ended as it had begun, against Australia, in 2004 while he called time on his domestic duties after the 2005-06 season with Harlequins.

Position	Centre
Country	England
Test span	1997–2004
Test caps	55
Lions caps	2
Test points	155 (31T)

MA'A NONU

MAJOR TEAMS: Wellington, Hurricanes, Ricoh Black Rams, Blues, Highlanders, Toulon, San Diego Legion, East Coast

There are precious few players who can lay an unequivocal claim to All Black greatness but Nonu is one who achieved such elusive status. His explosive international career spanned more than a decade and during his 12 years of muscular midfield service in the revered black shirt, the centre lifted the World Cup two times. Only 13 other Kiwis have ever been world champions twice.

His story began inauspiciously, debuting in the New Zealand team narrowly beaten by England in Wellington in 2003. It took him time to establish himself in the starting XV, but by the start of 2008 he was an automatic pick and an integral part of the All Blacks' plan to recapture the World Cup they agonisingly had not lifted since the inaugural tournament in 1987.

The 2011 edition of the competition on home soil saw Nonu feature in six of the side's seven outings. He scored the only Kiwi try in their 20-6 win over the Australians in the semi-final in Auckland and played every minute of the final, a tense 8-7 victory over France at Eden Park.

Four years later he was equally prominent, although this time he was on the scoresheet in the final itself, crossing the line early in the second-half against the Wallabies at Twickenham with an irresistible 40-metre burst to help steer New Zealand to a 34-17 win and back-to-back global triumphs. The 2015 final was Nonu's 103rd and final game for the All Blacks. Ninety-one of those games for his country yielded victories and he scored 31 tries in the process.

Blessed with the physique to punch holes in even the most miserly of defences, the centre's power belied his rugby intelligence and his ability to pick the most penetrating lines of attack. At the time he was only the sixth player to make 100 appearances for the All Blacks and to further burnish his international CV, he claimed five Rugby Championship titles and eight Bledisloe Cup victories.

Like many Kiwis, he spent the latter stages of his club career abroad, spending six seasons in France with Toulon, and was still playing professionally after his 40th birthday with the San Diego Legion side in America's MLR.

Position	Centre
Country	New Zealand
Test span	2003–2015
Test caps	103
Test points	155 (31T)

Kiwi powerhouse Nonu won two World Cups with the All Blacks during his glittering 12-year Test career

The grace of Bod O'Driscoll rips through Italy's defence during the 2014 Six Nations

MAJOR TEAMS: Leinster

Brian O'Driscoll – or Bod as he was dubbed – typified the unremitting valour that team-mates respect and supporters adore. Few players can touch his 141 caps, and only once – on his sixth appearance, against Romania – did Ireland's most legendary player not start the match.

He rarely left the field early either; on one occasion when he did, 55 minutes into the 2013 Dublin clash with the All Blacks after a tackle on Brodie Retallick left him concussed, Ireland famously let slip a 22-10 lead.

By that stage of his career O'Driscoll

BRIAN O'DRISCOLL

lacked the pace that had brought him so thrillingly to prominence with first, the hat-trick that defeated France in Paris in 2000 and then a glorious try for the 2001 Lions in Brisbane that sent the rapturous fans into choruses of *Waltzing O'Driscoll*.

Soon, the man whose first rugby experience had been as a tiny second-row for the Willow Park U12 fourth team was captaining his country, at the age of 23. He was to perform that duty with distinction on 83 occasions – only Richie McCaw and Sergio Parisse have skippered a country more often.

O'Driscoll's 47 Test tries – a record for both a centre and an Irishman – are all the more remarkable because of his astigmatism, which left him with only 50% of the average person's unaided vision. He had laser treatment in 2009 but had played 100-odd Tests by then – just think how good he would have been with proper eyesight!

When the zip in his running waned slightly, he compensated with his defence in the line and around rucks, his ability to spring to his feet and jackal the ball making him a king of the turnover.

Position	Centre
Country	Ireland
Test span	1999-2014
Ireland caps	133 (132 starts)
Lions caps	8 (8 starts)
Test points	250 (47T, 5DG)

He was a master of the interception score, so too the close-range burrowing snipe, yet his try-saving tackle on Scotland's Phil Godman in 2009 gave him as much satisfaction as any of his tries. It was instrumental in helping Ireland win the second of their three Grand Slams.

It was only fitting that this astonishing Dubliner – who strangely was never crowned World Player of the Year – bowed out internationally with a victory lap of honour in Paris as Ireland won the 2014 Six Nations. He has since become a highly respected pundit with BT Sport.

DANIE GERBER

MAJOR TEAMS: Eastern Province, Western Province

South Africa's spell in the sporting wilderness couldn't have come at a more inopportune time for Danie Gerber, who is hailed by many as his country's greatest-ever centre despite his relatively modest collection of caps.

Gerber, from the Eastern Province, emerged on the international scene in 1980, just missing that year's tour of South Africa by Bill Beaumont's Lions, and set about carving up opponents left, right and centre up until 1992.

Tragically, in sporting terms, he only won 24 caps – scoring 19 tries – when in any other era since he would have been close to three figures or beyond and setting almost unreachable scoring marks.

His most famous demolition job came in 1984 when he put England to the sword, scoring a try in a 33-15 victory in Port Elizabeth and a hat-trick in the second Test in Johannesburg when the Boks ran out 35-9 victors.

Gerber had tremendous power, good feet and acceleration, and according to his team-mate Ray Mordt was "the most dangerous player in the world from broken play". It was no wonder then that rugby league clubs in Britain were queueing up to sign the midfielder, but Gerber stayed as an amateur in union while Mordt and Rob Louw made the trek to Wigan.

When South Africa was reinstated into international rugby in 1992, Gerber, by now 34, scored two tries against the All Blacks in the Springboks' first match back in Johannesburg, but he retired from Test rugby after the defeat by England later that year. His career had featured appearances against sides like South America, the 1986 New Zealand Cavaliers and cobbled-together World XVs that did scant justice to his talents.

In 2007, Gerber was inducted into the International Rugby Hall of Fame – a small consolation for not being able to display his skills on a wider stage when he was in his prime. It was truly rugby's loss.

Position	Centre
Country	South Africa
Test span	1980-92
Test caps	24 (24 starts)
Test points	82 (19T, 1C)

One step ahead Gerber scores against France in Lyon, October 1992

TIM HORAN

Gold miner Horan sprints clear of the Springboks in 1999

MAJOR TEAMS: Queensland, Saracens

Is Tim Horan the greatest centre of all time? He's certainly a contender. As his boyhood pal and centre partner Jason Little told Australia's *Courier Mail* in 2014, "When we were together, they said we were the world's best centre pairing. I got dropped and Daniel Herbert came in, and they said he and Tim were the world's best. There was a common denominator there – and it wasn't me or Herbie."

Horan grew up in rural New South Wales, cut his rugby teeth at Toowoomba's Downlands College, joined the Queensland Reds set-up and won his first Test cap in August 1989, when he hadn't long turned 19.

When Horan scored two tries in his second game for Australia, away to France in 1989, coach Bob Dwyer knew he had found a diamond. Two years later Horan was a World Cup winner, scoring four tries in Australia's triumphant 1991 campaign.

Horan had great pace, a superb pass, was strong in defence and ran hard lines in attack, shredding the best defences in the world to score 30 Test tries and set up countless others.

His career was almost ended prematurely by a near-catastrophic knee injury suffered in the 1994 Super 10 final. Some experts didn't expect the 23-year-old to return, but he was back in time for his second World Cup in 1995.

Horan arguably peaked at RWC 1999 when he became one of an elite band to have won the Webb Ellis Cup twice and was named Player of the Tournament. He played a blinder in the Twickenham semi-final against South Africa having spent much of the previous 24 hours vomiting due to a vicious stomach bug.

Earlier in the tournament, he won a year's supply of Guinness and £10,000 for charity for scoring a try in less time than the brewer says it takes to pour the perfect pint (119 seconds – his try against Romania came after 92).

He played his last Test in 2000 having won nine of his 80 caps at fly-half and one on the wing, then shut the lid on his 114-cap Queensland career so he could join Saracens in England. Horan made more than 50 appearances for them before hanging up his boots in 2003.

Position	Centre
Country	Australia
Test span	1989-2000
England caps	80 (80 starts)
Test points	80 (80 starts)

RUGBY LEGENDS

FLY-HALVES

The so-called 'pretty boy' of the team, and the position to play if you crave attention. The fly-half calls the shots, deciding whether to kick the ball or pass it or have a dart himself. Play here and you must be a sea of serenity amid the turbulence around you, able to keep a cool head as you decide the actions needed to win the game. Almost always the main goalkicker, you will be targeted remorselessly in defence as the sight of a No 10 shirt gets up the nose of opposition ball-carriers. So be brave, be brilliant, and be ready to take the brickbats on those days when everything goes wrong.

NEIL JENKINS

MAJOR TEAMS: Pontypridd, Cardiff RFC, Celtic Warriors

Part of the fabric of Welsh rugby, first as a player and then as a coach after hanging up his unerringly accurate boots, Jenkins's prolific exploits are legendary and, although it is more than two decades since he last played international rugby, he remains the Principality's record points scorer. His historic haul of 1,049 points in red (not including the 41 he posted for the Lions) was, remarkably, achieved in a mere 87 Tests.

Aged 19 on debut against England in Cardiff in 1991, the fly-half was not the buccaneering 10 of earlier Welsh eras, but Jenkins was the rock on which the 1990s team was built. Deceptively quick and tactically astute, his ability to regularly dissect the uprights was unrivalled.

In 2001 he became the first player in the history of Test match rugby to smash through the fabled 1,000-point barrier, with his 28-point tally against the French in Paris. He set the unprecedented milestone in the Parc des Princes thanks to a 'full house' of try, conversion, penalty and drop goal in a rousing 43-35 triumph.

A veteran of Wales' 1995 and 1999 Rugby World Cup campaigns, his finest hour for his country came in 1994 when the side claimed the old Five Nations title. The Principality edged out England on points difference, Jenkins top scoring in the tournament with 48 to secure the coveted silverware for the first time in six years.

He toured with the Lions twice. Selected for the 1997 series in South Africa, the Welshman's presence was pivotal. In the first Test in Cape Town he landed five penalties from six as the Lions drew first blood at Newlands with a 25-16 victory, and only seven days later he was again on target with five penalties, as the Springboks were beaten in Durban and the tourists confirmed as series winners. He added 11 more points in the third match and finished the series as the Lions' top scorer.

A fourth cap for the Lions came in Australia in 2001, coming off the bench against the Wallabies in Melbourne. His final appearance for Wales was in late 2002, 11 years after his debut, against Romania in Wrexham.

Position	Fly-half
Country	Wales
Test span	1991–2002
Test caps	87
Lions caps	4
Test points	1,049 (11T, 130C, 235P, 10DG)

Points machine More than two decades after his retirement, Jenkins remains Wales's record points scorer

Raising the bar Wilkinson redefined what it means to be a professional

MAJOR TEAMS: Newcastle, Toulon

If Jonah Lomu shocked the world with his physical power, Jonny Wilkinson had no less of an impact with his sheer professionalism. Nobody in history has done more to prepare himself for a game of rugby, and scores of fellow pros were driven to raise their own standards having seen the English fly-half's obsessive training regime at close quarters.

Even as a lad, Wilkinson would rise early so he could practise kicking at his local club Farnham in Hampshire for 90 minutes before school. The hours paid

JONNY WILKINSON

Position	Fly-half
Country	England
Test span	1998-2011
England caps	91 (79 starts)
Lions caps	6 (6 starts)
Test points	1,246 (7T, 169C, 255P, 36DG)

off as he was to finish his career with a clatter of records, including most World Cup points (277), most Lions Test points (67) and most Test drop-goals (36).

England's youngest cap for 71 years when making his debut aged 18 in 1998, Wilkinson was initially an inside-centre before making the No 10 shirt his own by the age of 20. Among a multitude of outstanding performances, few match the one he gave off his sick bed in Bloemfontein in 2000, when he scored all the points in a 27-22 victory.

That South Africa tour gave England the belief they could beat anyone, and three years later Wilkinson dropped the goal that won the World Cup in Sydney.

His quest for perfection knew no bounds. A deadeye two-footed kicker and exquisite passer off both hands, he was also a remorseless and thumping tackler in a position that often sees reluctant and ineffectual defenders. He explained, "That ultra-competitive switch in me gets flicked when a ball-carrier looks at me as if to say 'I'm going to run straight over you'."

Against Ireland in England's emphatic 2003 Grand Slam win, he made three tackles in 22 seconds – not that we should be surprised because he regularly won the squad's conditioning tests. He was also struck by the footwork and agility of code-crosser Jason Robinson and sought to add those elements to his game.

Stardom sat uneasily on Wilkinson's shoulders and the Englishman endured a painful three years of 14 injuries and unwanted attention, his all-time worse situation being stuck on an EasyJet flight with a stag party chanting his name.

He returned to win another 42 caps, playing in two more World Cups, and after moving to France he guided Toulon to a domestic and European double before he retired. They even played *God Save The Queen* at the Top 14 final. "He's maybe the only English guy loved by all the French," said former team-mate Felipe Contepomi.

ANDREW MEHRTENS

MAJOR TEAMS: Canterbury, Crusaders, Harlequins, Toulon, Racing Métro 92, Béziers

Other international fly-halves have played more Tests and scored more points than Mehrtens, but none have entertained and enthralled to the same extent as the former All Blacks and Crusaders magician. Mehrtens was pure box office and lit up the pitch in a career with New Zealand which spanned nine years.

It began in Auckland against Canada in 1995. The 10 scored 28 points at Eden Park, a then world record for a debutant, a performance which earned him selection for the World Cup in South Africa later that year. Mehrtens was in the starting XV that narrowly lost the final 15-12 after extra time later that year, his late drop goal attempt inside the first 80 minutes with the scores level at 9-9 sailing agonisingly wide against the Springboks at Ellis Park.

Five years later there was solace for the fly-half when he became the All Blacks' record points scorer, surpassing the legendary Grant Fox's previous milestone mark of 645.

By the time his Test career was over in 2004, he had amassed 967 points with seven tries, 169 conversions, 188 penalties and 10 drop goals, which remains an All Blacks record, in his 70 international appearances. His incredible tally was subsequently overhauled by Dan Carter in 2009, but of all Test rugby's leading, all-time points scorers, whether they hail from New Zealand or further afield, none can rival Mehrtens points-per-game strike rate.

With the ability to split defences with his impressive range of passing, the playmaker enjoyed a stellar provincial career. Mehrtens was instrumental as the Crusaders were crowned Super Rugby champions four times in five years between 1998 and 2002, while in 2005 he became the competition's then record points accumulator. His finally tally of 990 points in Super Rugby was only eclipsed four years later.

Like many former All Blacks, he finished his playing career in Europe. His six seasons in the northern hemisphere saw no diminishment of his powers and in England with Harlequins and then in France with Toulon and Racing Metro he was instrumental in each club's promotion back to the top tier of their domestic leagues at the first time of asking.

Position	Fly-half
Country	New Zealand
Test span	1995–2004
Test caps	70
Test points	967 (7T,169C,188P, 10DG)

MARK ELLA

MAJOR TEAMS: Randwick, NSW, Milan

David Campese calls him the best he's ever seen and the only negative to Mark Ella's career was its brevity because, after blazing a trail across Australia and Europe, he quit the international game at the age of 25, seemingly unhappy at the more 'serious' approach imposed by Wallaby coach Alan Jones.

Ella was a one-off, a genius. Few players down the years could match his sublime ball-handling skills, but it was his attacking mindset that set him apart. Instead of defences looking to unnerve the fly-half, Ella turned the tables by putting pressure on defenders; he played so flat that they were forced to make decisions under stress. And by standing so close to his scrum-half – generally no more than three metres wide of him – he would draw the openside flanker onto him and take him out of the game.

Michael Lynagh, who played outside him on

Mesmeric Mark Ella

the 1984 Grand Slam tour, adopted much of Ella's teachings, including the 'catch, pass and support' principle that underpins classic running rugby.

"Mark would say that if he touched the ball twice the team tended to score and if he touched it three times he himself tended to score," Lynagh says. "His sleight of hand, his decoys and so forth, were mesmeric, and he was also a lovely communicator. He was great fun to play with."

On that 1984 European tour, Ella scored a try in every Test – replicating his achievement on the 1977-78 Australian Schoolboys tour – by following his pass and staying available as a support player. In tandem with brothers Glen and Gary, Mark Ella had set the Aussie club game alight when guiding Randwick to five consecutive Premierships from 1978-82. In the last of those years he was made Wallaby skipper – the first indigenous Australian to captain a national sports team.

He led his country in ten of his 25 Tests and his chilled-out character is highlighted by a tale told by former team-mate Michael Cheika, who recalls discovering Ella secretly listening to the races on an earpiece ahead of a comeback game by the fly-half in the late 1980s.

Ella played at Milan with Campese – a kindred spirit – before embarking on a coaching and media career.

Position	Fly-half
Country	Australia
Test span	1980-84
Test caps	25 (25 starts)
Test points	78 (6T, 3C, 8P, 8DG)

MICHAEL LYNAGH

Breaking Irish hearts Lynagh scores the last-gasp winner in the RWC 1991 quarter-final

MAJOR TEAMS: University of Queensland, Queensland, Saracens

As the son of a sports psychologist, Michael Lynagh paid close attention to mental preparation long before it was fashionable. On match days he would sit in the public areas of hotels so that people would talk to him and deny him the time to get nervous.

His strategies certainly worked because he retired from Test rugby as the world's record point-scorer with 911.

He was 21 when he played outside Mark Ella on the Wallabies' Grand Slam tour of 1984, and his distribution, measured tactical kicking and ability to never look rushed marked him out as a special talent.

By the 1991 World Cup he had become a world-class fly-half, and he showed in the closing minutes of the Ireland quarter-final that he possessed leadership skills to go with his clear thinking. Spurning a drop-goal attempt, he called a backs move that would win the game rather than draw it, and Lynagh himself went over for the crucial score. "Cometh the hour, cometh the man," said coach Bob Dwyer.

Nothing he did could match that day and the subsequent final victory over England, but he continued to impress on the highest stage right up to the last days of amateurism.

One of his finest days came in Paris in 1993 when, unencumbered by goalkicking duties, he orchestrated a sumptuous running display against the bewildered hosts. He signed off with 17 points in his final Test – one of 12 as Wallaby captain – against England at the 1995 World Cup.

Nicknamed 'Noddy', Lynagh then played three seasons in England with Saracens, culminating with victory in the 1998 Tetley's Bitter Cup final. In addition to his prodigious Test feats, he won 100 caps for Queensland, scoring 1,166 points.

Rugby World once played paintball with Lynagh and he splattered us in every game. His reactions were always a cut above and thank goodness he 'dodged a bullet' ten years ago when suffering a near fatal stroke. He's a staunch ally of the Stroke Association.

One of his greatest joys today is watching son Louis playing on the wing for Gallagher Premiership club Harlequins.

Position	Fly-half
Country	Australia
Test span	1984-95
Test caps	72 (71 starts)
Test points	911 (17T, 140C, 177P, 9DG)

BARRY JOHN

MAJOR TEAMS: Llanelli, Cardiff

It was the New Zealand press that coined Barry John's nickname – 'The King' – and the All Blacks were certainly subject to some of the fly-half's seminal displays over a fleeting but celebrated career.

Alongside Gareth Edwards he would become the scourge of the Kiwis, starting in 1967 when the duo combined to great effect for East Wales in a 3-3 draw.

John's gliding running style earned him Barbarians selection before four starts in the 1968 Five Nations and a place on the Lions tour to South Africa, where he broke his collarbone early in the first Test.

Injuries were a constant concern for John due to his slight frame, though two tries book-ended the 1969 Five Nations. Two years later he rubber-stamped a Welsh Grand Slam by ghosting through France's blind-side defence for a 9-5 victory.

That foreshadowed John's crowning glory, a starring role in the Lions' series success against the All Blacks. In the first Test in Dunedin he so tormented Fergie McCormick with his tactical kicking that the full-back never played for his country again, and a marvellous try – finishing off an Edwards break – paved the way for the 13-3 third-Test win in Wellington that ensured the Lions couldn't lose the series.

John made just as big a splash in the provincial fixtures, once taunting Hawke's Bay opponents by sitting on the ball in protest at their foul play.

Only John Dawes played more games than him on that tour and he finished with 194 points in 17 matches – a Lions record.

Two compatriots sum up John's rare gifts. Gerald Davies suggested "the game would bend to his will and no one else's", while Cliff Morgan said: "Like all great ball players, Pelé and Best, Compton and Sobers, Barry looked as if he had plenty of time to do things. It seemed easy for him."

John walked away in 1972, consumed by the claustrophobia of public adoration. After a cashier curtsied to him at a bank, he decided to retire in order to escape the 'goldfish bowl'. Only 27, he had forged a prodigious legacy.

Position	Fly-half
Country	Wales
Test span	1966-72
Wales caps	25 (25 starts)
Lions caps	5 (5 starts)
Test points	120 (6T, 9C, 18P, 10DG)

Holding court John was at his imperious best on the fields of New Zealand

DAN CARTER

Man for the big occasion Carter celebrates winning the 2015 World Cup. He kicked 19 points in the final

MAJOR TEAMS: Canterbury, Crusaders, Perpignan, Racing, Kobelco Steelers

Pound for pound, Dan Carter is thought by many to be the finest outside-half ever to have graced the game. As a kicker, he had few peers. He amassed more than 3,000 points in the Test and domestic arena, is the world's top international point-scorer and crossed the whitewash on 29 occasions.

After progressing through the age grades, Carter made his full debut at 21 at centre against Wales, scoring 20 points, before vying with Carlos Spencer for the No 10 shirt at the 2003 World Cup.

He made the fly-half spot his own the following year and in 2005 led the All Blacks to a Lions series whitewash, playing what was thought to be the 'perfect' game in the second Test in Wellington, when his 33-point haul included two tries and a bewitching array of skills. His game management, broken-field running and unerring boot simply overwhelmed Sir Clive Woodward's flummoxed charges.

Carter's talent saw him win the highest individual honour in the game on three occasions, being named World Player of the Year in 2005, 2012 and 2015.

Not everything was plain sailing for Carter, who endured a few bumps in World Cups. After a shock exit in 2007, where he was injured against France in the quarter-finals, he was again crocked in 2011 after a torn adductor in training forced him to miss the knockout stage.

Salvation came in 2015 when he steered the All Blacks to back-to-back world titles, slotting a magnificent drop-goal when the team was wobbling in the final against Australia. "He had the capacity to figure out on the run what to do ahead of everyone else. He played the moment," said the great Irish ten Ronan O'Gara.

Commentator Scotty Stevenson is another admirer, saying, "There was a grace about Dan Carter. There was a glorious choreography about how he approached playing football. It was like watching an illusionist."

Carter enjoyed spells in France and Japan before retiring from pro rugby last year. His place in the pantheon is assured.

Position	Fly-half
Country	New Zealand
Test span	2003-15
Test caps	112 (106 starts)
Test points	1,598 (29T, 293C, 281P, 8DG)

PHIL BENNETT

MAJOR TEAMS: Llanelli

How many pints of Brains beer have been sunk while Welsh fans have debated whether Phil Bennett or Barry John is the greatest fly-half the world has ever seen? Thousands, no doubt, as it has been one of rugby's favourite discussion points.

Those in the Bennett camp cite the Llanelli man's part in the unbeaten Lions tour of 1974 and his magical series of sidesteps that started the length-of-pitch move for Gareth Edwards's breathtaking Barbarians try against New Zealand.

Certainly, Bennett's footwork was unparalleled. Half-back partner Edwards said he was "a fantastic stepper but sometimes I think even Phil didn't know where his sidesteps would take him".

Talking to *The Daily Telegraph*, Edwards also dubbed the former steelworker "an instinctive genius", and anyone who saw Bennett's performance in the second Lions Test against South Africa in 1974 couldn't disagree. The maestro had the game of his life, creating tries for his team-mates in a 28-9 drubbing and scoring a brilliant one himself with a trademark sidestepping run from deep.

A leg injury almost ended his tour at that juncture, but skipper Willie John McBride was so against Bennett going home that he carried him around for the next few days to help him heal. Bennett, unable to run properly in the third Test as his legs were numb with painkillers, dropped two goals as the series was clinched in Port Elizabeth.

Bennett made his Wales debut aged 20 as the nation's first Test replacement but didn't secure the No 10 jersey until John retired in 1972. He had his down times too; he briefly lost his place to John Bevan and later floundered under the pressure of the Lions captaincy on the rain-plagued 1977 tour to New Zealand, which the tourists lost 3-1 after almost drawing the series.

He led Wales eight times from 1977 and his Test career finished with a flourish in 1978 as he scored two tries in a 16-7 win over France to bag a second Grand Slam. He was awarded an OBE the next year.

Cheers! Bennett toasts a *Rugby World* Player of the Year award

Position	Fly-half
Country	Wales
Test span	1969-78
Wales caps	29 (26 starts)
Lions caps	8 (8 starts)
Test points	210 (5T, 20C, 46P, 4DG)

BEAUDEN BARRETT

MAJOR TEAMS: Hurricanes, Blues, Suntory Sungoliath, Toyota Verblitz

The embodiment of the perfect player: fast, skilful, daring, exhilarating. Barrett played bare-footed with his brothers until the age of ten – "It was awesome because you felt really quick" – and it's as if he has transported those carefree days to the Test arena. He's not a player to die wondering and so much of what he tries comes off, from audacious kick-passes to reverse offloads and even one-handed pick-ups. Quick enough to shame most international wingers, Barrett's ability to see the space and exploit it with searing acceleration has ripped holes in all of the world's best defences. And that works the other way, as we saw when he scored two interception tries against Wales on his 100th New Zealand appearance in 2021. "He's got that freakish ability to defend two spaces because he knows he's got the speed to make up for it," said All Blacks coach Ian Foster. "If you look at all his qualities, the ability to run fast and be decisive are probably his greatest." Speed of foot, speed of thought – it's a deadly combination and quite apart from the avalanche of Test tries this twice World Rugby Player of the Year has created for others, Barrett has scored 45 of his own, placing him third on the All-Blacks Test points-scoring list, over a decade since he made his Test debut in a 60-0 rout of Ireland in 2012. International rugby must have seemed easy, as he was on the winning side in his first 19 Tests and became a world champion from the bench when New Zealand beat the Wallabies at Twickenham in the final of the 2015 World Cup.

Position	Fly-half
Country	New Zealand
Test span	2012-
Test caps	134
Test points	772 (45T, 179C, 60P, 3DG)

HUGO PORTA

MAJOR TEAMS: Banco Nación

Has any player done more to elevate rugby from a minor to a major sport in their own country than Hugo Porta in Argentina?

His first dozen caps in 1971-73 came against South American nations, an unofficial South Africa team, Romania and an Ireland XV, but over the next 12 years Porta's talent persuaded the likes of Australia, France, New Zealand and England to play full Tests against the Pumas, initiating their climb to rugby's top table.

Porta was 20 when he made his debut against Chile and 39 when he won his final cap – although he played once more in 1999 against a World XV!

A pinpoint kicker, Porta is Argentina's third-highest Test point-scorer with 590, he also had silky handling skills and loved creative, running play. He was a great leader, captaining Argentina from 1977 to his first retirement in 1987, and then for three more Tests on his comeback in 1990.

Porta became a national icon in a country obsessed by football, having turned down an approach by soccer club Boca Juniors in his youth. He led the South American Jaguars (a composite side) eight times in the early 1980s, while perhaps his greatest performance came in 1985, when he kicked all 21 points in Argentina's landmark draw against the All Blacks.

His achievements – which included 28 Test drop goals, second only to Jonny Wilkinson – were recognised by World Rugby in 2008 when he was inducted into their Hall of Fame. Before that, in 1985, readers of French paper *Midi Olympique* voted him the world's best player and he was Argentine Sportsman of the Year that year – extraordinary, considering football's status in his homeland.

A qualified architect, Porta's career took a different path after rugby and he became Argentina's ambassador to South Africa in 1991, sports minister from 1994-99 and joined the Argentine union in 2006.

Position	Fly-half
Country	Argentina
Test span	1971-90
Argentina caps	58 (58 starts)
S America caps	8 (8 starts)
Test points	651 (12T, 90C, 114P, 28DG)

Hugo that way Porta throws a sidestep during a match in Dublin. The Puma played Test rugby until the age of 39

OWEN FARRELL

MAJOR TEAMS: Saracens, Racing 92

Over the past decade and a half, the name Owen Farrell has become synonymous with English rugby success. Not only has he thrived at the club level, winning numerous titles with Saracens, including five Premiership titles and three European Champions Cups, but his international career has made him a household name. His international accolades include winning the Six Nations title in 2016, 2017 and 2020 as well as captaining England to a Rugby World Cup final in 2019. Farrell is known for his exceptional leadership skills and his accuracy in kicking. With over 100 caps with the English team, and over 1,200 points during his international test career, only Dan Carter has scored more in international rugby. This is a testament not only to his undeniable talent, but also to the drive and longevity that have kept him at the forefront of the game since 2008. He has won many individual accolades throughout his career, including the Rugby Players' Association Player of the Year award in 2018 and the Premiership Rugby Player of the Season award in 2019. In addition to his club and international career, Farrell has also represented the British and Irish Lions on three tours, in 2013, 2017 and 2021. He went into self-imposed international exile in the summer of 2024 when he signed for French side Racing 92, ruling himself out of selection for the Red Rose, but has not officially retired from Test rugby and if he returned to the Premiership, could yet add to his record-breaking England points tally.

Position	Fly-half
Country	England
Test span	2012-
Test caps	112
Lions caps	6 (3 starts)
Test points	1,237 (10T, 199C, 258P, 5DG)

Playmaker Farrell is a masterful tactical kicker

JOHNNY SEXTON

Old reliable At 37, Sexton has established himself as one of Ireland's greats

MAJOR TEAMS: Leinster, Racing 92

Johnny Sexton established himself as one of the best fly-halves of his generation during his glittering 14 years on the international stage. Sexton's Test career has been nothing short of remarkable. He has played a key role in Ireland's successes over the past decade, including their Grand Slam victories in the 2018 and 2023 Six Nations Championships. In the 2023 Six Nations, Sexton became the highest scoring player ever in the competition, overtaking his old teammate Ronan O'Gara. Sexton has also been a crucial player for the British and Irish Lions, featuring in the 2013, 2017, and 2021 tours, and scoring the winning drop goal in the third test against Australia in 2013. Sexton is known for his accurate goal-kicking, his ability to control a game with his tactical kicking, and his bravery in defence. He has also demonstrated his leadership skills, having captained both Leinster and Ireland on numerous occasions. Despite his success, Sexton has had to overcome several setbacks, including injuries that have threatened to derail his career. His final appearance for Ireland came in the 2023 World Cup quarter-final against the All Blacks in Paris, ending his career as his country's all-time leading points scorer and the fourth most prolific player in Test match history.

Position	Fly-half
Country	Ireland
Test span	2009–2023
Test caps	118
Lions caps	6 (5 starts)
Test points	1,108 (18T, 182C, 214P, 4DG)

DAN BIGGAR

Mainstay Biggar has been a rock for Wales

Ospreys, Northampton Saints, Toulon

Dan Biggar is a Welsh rugby union player who is widely regarded as one of the best fly-halves in the world. Although the Welsh national team have oftentimes rotated kickers, Biggar has been a mainstay in the national team for the last decade and a half. Biggar made his debut for the Welsh national team in 2008 and quickly became a regular starter. He played a key role in the team's successful Six Nations campaigns in 2012, 2013, 2019 and 2021, helping Wales secure Grand Slam titles on two of those occasions. Biggar's skill, precision, and composure on the pitch have made him one of the most respected fly-halves in world rugby. He is known for his ability to control a game with his kicking and passing skills, and his tenacity in defence. In 2015, Biggar played a crucial role in Wales' run to the Rugby World Cup quarter-finals, where they were eventually defeated by South Africa. He was named the Man of the Match in the team's narrow victory over England in the group stage, thanks to his accurate kicking and composure under pressure.

Position	Fly-half
Country	Wales
Test span	2008–2023
Test caps	112
Lions caps	3 (3 starts)
Test points	633 (8T, 103C, 120P, 9DG)

RONAN O'GARA

MAJOR TEAMS: Munster

Ronan O'Gara is an Irish former rugby union player who is widely regarded as one of the greatest fly-halves in the history of the sport. O'Gara made his debut for the Irish national team in 2000, and went on to earn 128 caps over the course of his career. He was a key player for Ireland for over a decade, and was instrumental in helping the team win the Six Nations championship in 2009 and 2014. His drop goal in the 77th minute of the winner-takes-all game against Wales in 2009 is certainly one for the highlight reel, and secured Ireland's first Grand Slam win in 61 years. O'Gara's skill and creativity on the pitch have made him a standout player at both the international and club levels. He spent the majority of his club career playing for Munster in Ireland, where he won numerous domestic and European titles, including the European Champions Cup twice. O'Gara's kicking skills are particularly renowned, and he is considered one of the greatest goal-kickers in the history of the sport. He also has a keen tactical mind and is known for his ability to control a game with his passing and decision-making. After retiring from playing in 2013, O'Gara moved into coaching, taking up a position as an assistant coach at Racing 92 in France. He later joined Crusaders in New Zealand as a backs coach and joined La Rochelle in the Top 14 as head coach in 2019 where his team won the Champions Cup final in 2022. In 2023 he coached Stade Rochelaise to another famous Champions Cup Final victory over the favourites Leinster at the Aviva Stadium in Dublin winning 27-26. This speaks volumes regarding his on-field intellect, as the transition from player to coach is not a road much travelled, and for good reason. In addition to his success on the pitch, O'Gara has also earned numerous accolades for his contributions to the sport. He was inducted into the World Rugby Hall of Fame in 2021, and was also awarded the Rugby Writers of Ireland Player of the Year award on three occasions.

Position	Fly-half
Country	Ireland
Test span	1997-2013
Ireland caps	128 (87 starts)
Lions caps	2 (0 starts)
Test points	1083 (16T, 176C, 202P, 15DG)

Sharp tack O'Gara is one of the brightest minds in the game

RUGBY LEGENDS

SCRUM-HALVES

Scrum-halves shouldn't count sheep in their sleep – they should count the number of passes they've hopefully made in that week's training. And it should run to hundreds, because they need to deliver rapid and accurate service to their fly-half off both hands. But a good No 9 must also be willing to snipe himself or link with his back row – keeping the defence guessing. A towering box-kick is mandatory and if you're not one of the gobbiest members of the team you're in the wrong job, because communication is critical. This role is made for a bossy boots!

AIG

GARY ARMSTRONG

MAJOR TEAMS: Jed-Forest, Newcastle Falcons, Borders

"Inside me at scrum-half I have one of the toughest players in the world. We call Gary Armstrong the Junkyard Dog."

Those were the words of Jonny Wilkinson on his former Newcastle team-mate. He wasn't the only man to praise the Jeddart great's ticker. Former Scotland coach Jim Telfer, no stranger to pain himself, once said Armstrong had an inhuman tolerance of pain. And David Sole, captain of the 1990 Grand Slam team, said: "If you were picking one guy to go over the top you would pick Gary Armstrong. He was a phenomenal player with incredible courage." Ask many a Borderer who their childhood hero was and Armstrong's name bursts out, closely followed by the word "mental".

Armstrong epitomised everything that was great about amateurism in rugby. He was a long-haul lorry driver as well as a snapping terrier of a scrum-half who took contact unflinchingly. He was a Lions tourist in 1989 and seen as one of the best No 9s in the world in the mid-1990s while working gruelling hours.

He eventually answered the siren's call of professionalism, leaving Scotland to play seven seasons in Newcastle from 1997, winning the Premiership title in his first term. However, he jokes that he only learned to pass off his left hand once he was paid to play.

Longevity twinned with a willingness to grit his teeth and get on with it endeared him to supporters. It was a huge shame that he missed the 1995 World Cup because of a knee injury, but Armstrong still managed to play in World Cups in 1991 and 1999, star in the famous Grand Slam team of 1990 and nine years later captain Scotland to the last-ever Five Nations title.

He returned to his homeland in 2002 to play for the professional Borders side for two years before calling it a day.

Scotland have developed a long line of sensational scrum-halves over the years, but Armstrong was one of the most dedicated and respected.

Position	Scrum-half
Country	Scotland
Test span	1988-99
Test caps	51 (49 starts)
Test points	21 (5T)

Border terrier Armstrong possessed an "inhuman tolerance of pain"

WILL GENIA

MAJOR TEAMS: Reds, Stade Français, Rebels, Kintetsu Liners

Following in the footsteps of George Gregan as the Wallabies' number nine never fazed Genia. Gregan's international career was iconic, not least his legacy as Test rugby's most capped scrum-half of all time, but Genia emerged from his predecessor's shadow to become an Australian legend.

A livewire half-back with mesmeric balance and fast hands, Genia was introduced to the sport at the age of 12 when he left Papua New Guinea, and by the age of 21 he was a Test player after his debut against New Zealand in Auckland.

By 2011 he was proudly wearing the captain's armband for his adopted country in the World Cup clash with the USA in Wellington, and subsequently made the shortlist for the World Rugby Player of the Year Award.

A constant threat around the edges of ruck or maul, Genia started all three Tests against the Lions in 2013 and two years later was in the starting XV beaten by the All Blacks in the World Cup final at Twickenham.

The home of English rugby, however, yielded happier memories in late 2018 when Genia became only the 10th ever Wallaby to amass 100 caps. The 2019 Rugby World Cup was his third and final appearance in the tournament as Genia called time on his international career and headed to Japan to play for the Kintetsu Liners club.

Still sniping around the fringes into his late 30s, Genia claimed two career Rugby Championship titles with Australia in 2011, starting all four fixtures, and again in 2015, the Wallabies' most recent success in the annual battle for southern hemisphere supremacy.

Position	Scrum-half
Country	Australia
Test span	2009–2019
Test caps	110
Test points	90 (18T)

NICK FARR-JONES

MAJOR TEAMS: Sydney University, NSW

Nick Farr-Jones was part of the Wallabies' 'Holy Trinity' alongside Michael Lynagh and David Campese. Indeed, it was even said that the quick-thinking, cerebral No 9 created 46 of Campo's 64 Test tries.

Brought up in Sydney, Farr-Jones made his debut on the 1984 Grand Slam tour. Two years later he was key to Australia's triumph in New Zealand; his performance into a gale in Wellington – with blindside snipes and smart interchanges with the forwards – was a joy to behold.

Despite a disappointing fourth-place finish at the 1987 World Cup, Farr-Jones had a fine tournament dictating his team's tempo and was soon chosen by Bob Dwyer to captain the team.

In the first Test against the 1989 Lions he gave another model demonstration of half-back play. Lions hooker Brian Moore said in his book Beware of the Dog, "Farr-Jones's distribution was swift, he knew when to take on the back row and especially when not to throw out rubbish. No one has ever played the perfect game, but they (Farr-Jones and Lynagh) made so few errors that it was pretty close to ideal."

Yet the Lions hit back to win the series and Farr-Jones had a notorious dust-up with Robert Jones after being provoked.

Despite his captaincy being scrutinised, he skippered his side to a 21-9 win in the Bledisloe Cup, which led to him famously taking a naked swim in Wellington Harbour.

At the 1991 World Cup, Farr-Jones drove his team to defeat the All Blacks in the semi-finals. "We had to tackle till our shoulders were red-raw just to keep them out," he said, before going on to lift the trophy at Twickenham with a 12-6 win over England.

He and Lynagh played 47 Tests together and Farr-Jones finished with a then world record 36 Tests as captain. He also captained a World XV in three Tests against New Zealand. After a brief retirement, he was persuaded into playing a final winning series against South Africa.

A lawyer for a decade, Farr-Jones then moved into investment management. He also served as chairman of NSW Rugby and created his own charity, Touch Life, to support the homeless.

Position	Scrum-half
Country	Australia
Test span	1984-93
Test caps	63 (62 starts)
Test points	37 (9T)

Royal command Farr-Jones, one of only two backs to lead a World Cup-winning XV, receives the trophy in 1991

JUSTIN MARSHALL

MAJOR TEAMS: Canterbury, Crusaders, Leeds, Ospreys, Montpellier, Saracens

France, at the old Parc des Princes, is nobody's idea of an easy Test debut but Laurie Mains had a clear motive for giving Justin Marshall his All Black bow there on the 1995 European tour. "The French were really aggressive in the rucks and mauls," the coach said, "and we needed Justin's ruggedness."

There are more skilful players in our No 9s list than Marshall but no one more competitive and ready to scrap than the small-town boy from Mataura, near Invercargill, who became New Zealand's most-capped scrum-half (before current choice Aaron Smith overtook him).

Beginning working life as a butcher, Marshall showed an impeccable sense of timing because All Blacks incumbents Graeme Bachop and Ant Strachan both left for Japan in 1995 – opening the door for Marshall at the start of the pro era.

His physicality and explosive speed around the fringes, where he liked to use players around him to manipulate the defence, made him an instant fit in an All Black team that dominated world rugby. As impressive as anything were his organising and communication, his Canterbury coach Aussie McLean once saying, "People just don't realise the influence he has out there. He runs everything on defence."

Marshall played 23 consecutive Tests from his Paris debut until a snapped Achilles interrupted the run, although, as an insatiable trainer, he was back in action two months ahead of schedule.

He didn't have selection all his own way, being ousted by Byron Kelleher for the RWC 1999 semi-final. Responding to criticism that his pass was slow, he points to the speed with which he got the ball away from the breakdown, and certainly his half-back partner, Andrew Mehrtens, never looked short of time.

Appointed ABs captain in 1997, Marshall soon lost the job for upsetting a referee. But he went on starring for his country until 2005, beating the Lions and finishing with 24 Test tries before a European swansong. He's now an analyst for Sky Sports.

Position	Scrum-half
Country	New Zealand
Test span	1995-2005
Ireland caps	81 (74 starts)
Test points	120 (24T)

Big personality Marshall on the burst for Crusaders. "He's an exclamation mark, not a comma," said wife Nicolle

Maestro in mid-flight Edwards moves the ball during Wales' victory against Ireland in 1975

MAJOR TEAMS: Cardiff

Gareth Edwards wanted to be a centre like his hero Bleddyn Williams, but at 5ft 3in and 8st 5lb, he was taken off during a district U15 trial to prevent him getting hurt. He was simply too small.

PE teacher Bill Samuel persuaded him that the scrum-half position would suit him better, and for that intervention – along with his determination to secure Edwards a sports scholarship to Millfield School when the youngster was set to become a soccer professional with Swansea City – rugby will forever be in

GARETH EDWARDS

the late Samuel's debt.

Edwards became one of the sporting greats, not just a rugby legend. He played for Wales at 19, captained them at 20 and won 53 consecutive caps during a decade of dazzling brilliance. Only five men have played more Tests for the British & Irish Lions.

The teenage Edwards developed into a sensational athlete. His school had only one hurdle yet he became Welsh Schools champion in both hurdling and long jump.

The best players possess exceptional drive and he spent hours perfecting his pass, using a sand-filled ball to develop distance and passing through a swinging tyre to sharpen his reflexes.

Some of the game's greatest moments have Edwards at their core, such as the 1973 try he scored for the Baa-Baas or the solo try against Scotland in the mud that highlighted his speed, power, skill and mental courage.

He played every Test of the victorious Lions tours of 1971 and 1974, and it's often forgotten that the latter tourists, celebrated as invincibles, were seconds away from losing to Orange Free State when Edwards conjured the winning try with a magical over-the-head pass to JJ Williams.

Position	Scrum-half
Country	Wales
Test span	1967-78
Wales caps	53 (53 starts)
Lions caps	10 (10 starts)
Test points	91 (20T, 2C, 1P, 4DG)

Numerous rugby luminaries don't hesitate to name Edwards as the greatest ever, with former England captain Will Carling once writing, "He was outstanding at running, passing, kicking and reading the game. He played in the 1970s but if he played now he would still be the best."

Knighted in 2015, Sir Gareth has so far set standards that arguably no one else in the sport can reach.

AGUSTÍN PICHOT

MAJOR TEAMS: Club Atlético San Isidro, Richmond, Bristol, Stade Français, Racing

In the immediate aftermath of Argentina's maiden Rugby Championship triumph in 2014 – a tense 21-17 defeat of Australia in Mendoza – emotions were running high. Even so, mercurial centre Juan Martin Hernández had one figure in mind above all else. "Many people were involved in making this dream come true,' he said. "But I want to dedicate this victory to Agustín."

The tribute was touching, not least because Agustín Pichot spent his entire career as an insatiable standard-driver. That role seemed to be magnified by the intensity of the international arena, and he became an icon of the 2007 World Cup.

Shoulder-length hair tousled around his collar and socks rolled down around the ankles, captain Pichot stood in the centre of a circle of team-mates before and after each match. He spoke with conviction, cajoling them to work harder, congratulating them for challenging the world order.

By the end of the tournament, Argentina had defeated Ireland, Scotland and France twice en route to third place. To precurse his impact as a major campaigner post retirement – pivotal in introducing Argentina to the Rugby Championship and a South American franchise to Super Rugby – Pichot underlined his talents as a magnificent scrum-half.

In possession, he probed around the fringes, pulling defenders around and releasing carriers. Without the ball, he harried runners relentlessly.

Pichot was just 20 when he made a try-scoring Test debut against Australia in 1995 and remained with Buenos Aires amateur outfit Club Atlético San Isidro until joining Richmond in 1997. Via an enjoyable stint at Bristol, he arrived at Stade Français in 2003 and helped them to domestic titles in 2004 and 2007.

In 2000, Pichot captained Argentina for the first time in a 34-23 success over Ireland, and he was subsequently involved in overturning every Six Nations side, most notably England at Twickenham by 25-18 in 2006.

Speaking about the notion of Argentina one day winning the Rugby Championship, he crystallised his own ambitious philosophy. "We're going for that, full throttle. Let's dream." And why not?

Pichot stood for election as World Rugby chairman in 2020, losing narrowly to the incumbent, Bill Beaumont.

Position	Scrum-half
Country	Argentina
Test span	1995-2007
Test caps	71 (69 starts)
Test points	60 (12T)

Laser focus Pichot in action at the 2007 World Cup

AARON SMITH

MAJOR TEAMS: Highlanders

Sleight of hand Smith fires out one of his lightning passes

The past 12 months has seen a number of milestones for Aaron Smith. He broke the record for the most Highlanders appearances in March 2021, surpassing Ben Smith's mark of 153. He won his 100th cap last August, helping the All Blacks to retain the Bledisloe Cup with back-to-back wins against the Wallabies. Then he welcomed his second child in November, the spell of paternity delaying his arrival on his country's European tour.

Now 33, he has been overtaken, in *Rugby World*'s humble opinion, by Antoine Dupont in the current scrum-half stakes. Smith has proved an irresistible force from the moment the then Test newcomer played a central role in the All Blacks' 3-0 series win over Ireland in 2012.

Fast ball is everything in rugby and the quality of Smith's delivery from the base separates him from every nine on the planet – Dupont included. "His pass is by far the best in the world by a half-back," Wallaby Tate McDermott told us. "He's probably the best scrum-half passer of a ball that we've ever had," said England veteran Danny Care.

It's Smith's wrists that largely account for his lightning pass, his lack of a wind-up or swing of the arms providing precious extra split-seconds for his team-mates to play from. Couple this with his perpetual motion, lethal running, clever kicking game and sharp brain and you have one of the greatest players of the century.

A Super Rugby champion in 2015, Smith overtook Justin Marshall to become New Zealand's most-capped No 9 in 2018 and led them for the first time in July 2021 against Fiji. He is a fly-half's dream, the "loquacious chauffeur" during a golden period for the All Blacks, to cite analyst Stuart Barnes.

"I feel better now than I did in my late twenties," Smith said ahead of becoming a Test centurion. "The top two inches is easy around getting mentally ready for things, but physically it's just hard work. There is no substitution. You earn everything you get."

Position	Scrum-half
Country	New Zealand
Test span	2012-
Test caps	102 (94 starts)
Test points	107 (21T, 1C)

KEN CATCHPOLE

MAJOR TEAMS: Randwick, NSW

It's hard to know where to begin when listing the achievements of Ken Catchpole.

He captained Australia on his Test debut and 12 other occasions, was heralded by Dudley Harrison, the RFU president in 1966, as "the greatest half-back the world has known", and was inducted into the Hall of Fame at Twickenham in 2004, the new Australia Rugby Union equivalent in 2005 and the IRB (now World Rugby) Hall of Fame in 2013. You might say he is a legend among the legends in these pages.

The Sydney-born Catchpole joined the Randwick club and made his NSW debut

Position	Scrum-half
Country	Australia
Test span	1961-68
Test caps	27 (27 starts)
Test points	9 (3T)

against the touring Lions in 1959, aged just 19.

Two years later he captained Australia during a three-Test series against Fiji – the ninth player to lead a Test side on debut – and over the ensuing eight years he formed a ground-breaking half-back combination with Phil Hawthorne. The sharp service they offered set up many a famous victory during the 1960s and produced a change in style from an age when the backs had spread across the width of the pitch, as this pair employed more short passes and Catchpole used his speed off the mark to cut through defences.

He was in his pomp in back-to-back wins over South Africa in 1965 and on a tour of Europe in 1966-67, when he captained the Wallabies once more and guided them to a then record 23-11 win over England.

His career came to a premature end just before his 29th birthday when All Blacks lock Colin Meads tried to drag him out of a ruck by one leg – unaware that Catchpole's other leg was trapped. The unfortunate Australian suffered horrific injuries, tearing his hamstring from the bone and rupturing his groin.

Club players in NSW still know his name well, as every year they vie for the Ken Catchpole Medal, awarded to the winner of a season-long vote by referees.

GEORGE GREGAN

MAJOR TEAMS: Brumbies, Toulon, Suntory Sungoliath

In the dying seconds of the deciding Test against Australia in Sydney 21 years ago, the British & Irish Lions still had a shot of snatching the series. Though trailing 29-23, they had possession and were stretching their opponents.

Then a pass went loose. Wallaby wing Andrew Walker scooped it up and walked over the touchline to end the game. George Gregan stood metres away. The scrum-half had played every minute of three high-octane encounters. He mimed a pistol with the first two fingers on his right hand, held the imaginary gun to his lips and blew the imaginary smoke away.

Similarly spiky bravado surfaced two years later in the same arena. Australia led New Zealand 22-10 in a semi-final. Sure of a spot in the World Cup final, they were awarded a breakdown penalty. Leaning over the ruck, captain Gregan delivered the immortal sledge, "Four more years, boys. Four more years."

The Aussies lost the final but Gregan was by then ensconced as his nation's talisman.

Back in 1994, just four matches into a 139-cap Test career, the then 21-year-old wrote himself into Bledisloe Cup legend with a stunning try-saving tackle on All Black wing Jeff Wilson. Australia won 20-16.

As in 2003, Gregan's first and last World Cups in 1995 and 2007 would end in a knockout loss to England. However, his precise distribution and mathematical game management in tandem with fly-half Stephen Larkham, including a defence-splitting reverse pass, reaped rewards in the interim.

That superb half-back pairing appeared together 79 times for Australia and helped the Brumbies to two Super 12 titles.

Fierce dedication was a cornerstone of Zambia-born Gregan's longevity, and he spent his twilight years between Toulon and Japanese side Suntory Sungoliath.

Eddie Jones summed up Gregan's achievements when the player reached 100 Tests in 2004. "Anyone who plays 100 caps at 80 kilos has got to have something going for him," he said. "He's just got incredible mental focus."

King George No Australian has won as many caps as Gregan

Position	Scrum-half
Country	Australia
Test span	1994-2007
Test caps	139 (133 starts)
Test points	99 (18T, 3DG)

JOOST VAN DER WESTHUIZEN

MAJOR TEAMS: Blue Bulls

When Gareth Edwards was knighted in 2015, rugby pundits tried to come up with the name of a scrum-half who could have lived with the mighty Welshman. For many, Joost van der Westhuizen's was the only name in the frame.

The South African had the lot. He was fast and fearless, could break the line, had a strong pass and tackled himself into the ground, never more than when he brought down Jonah Lomu in the RWC 1995 final.

Like Edwards, van der Westhuizen also had an eye for the line as 38 tries in his 89 Tests prove. By the time he retired after the 2003 World Cup he was South Africa's most-capped player and record try-scorer. Although those marks have both been eclipsed, his contribution to his country has never been forgotten.

Van der Westhuizen should have had a long and happy retirement ahead of him. He was a World Cup winner, a legend at the Bulls, had earned a degree in commerce and was one of the most recognisable rugby players on the planet.

A few lurid tales hit the press but the South African – who had been inducted into the Hall of Fame in 2007 – rode the storm before he was confronted by his biggest opponent in 2011. At the age of 40, he was diagnosed with amyotrophic lateral sclerosis – a form of motor neurone disease. He was given between two and five years to live and fought the disease with the same appetite he showed for taking the fight to opponents on the field.

Van der Westhuizen threw his weight behind raising awareness of MND and in 2013 travelled to Cardiff ahead of South Africa's November Test against Wales. Edwards was there to meet him, a fitting meeting of two legendary half-backs.

Van der Westhuizen died in 2017, aged 45. Former Boks captain Corne Krige said, "If you wanted an X-factor in your team, he was that guy. He was the ultimate modern-day scrum-half – the first of the bigger scrum-halves in the world."

Position	Scrum-half
Country	South Africa
Test span	1993–2003
Test caps	89 (78 starts)
Test points	190 (38T)

Joost amazing Launching a diving pass on his final Test appearance, 2003

ANTOINE DUPONT

MAJOR TEAMS: Castres, Toulouse

Antoine Dupont is a French rugby union player who has arguably established himself as the best current scrum half in world rugby. Dupont's breakthrough season came in 2017 when he helped Castres win the Top 14 title, earning himself the Young Player of the Year award in the process. His performances for Castres earned him a call-up to the French national team in 2017, and he made his debut against Italy in the 2017 Six Nations Championship.

Antoine Dupont's international career has been nothing short of spectacular. He has become a key player for France, guiding them to an unbeaten 2022 calendar year, which included their first Six Nations win since 2010. Dupont's speed, agility, and vision on the pitch have earned him comparisons to former French scrum half Fabien Galthié. Dupont is known for his ability to create scoring opportunities for his teammates, his quick thinking and sharp passing skills, and his physicality in defence.

He has become a fan favourite in France and is widely regarded as one of the most exciting players to watch in world rugby. In 2021, Dupont was named the Six Nations Player of the Championship, becoming the first French player to win the award since its inception in 2004. He also helped France secure their first win against New Zealand in over a decade, scoring a try in the process.

At just 28 years old, Dupont has already achieved a great deal in his rugby career and although there was disappointment in the 2023 Rugby World Cup when Les Bleus fell at the quarter-final stage on home soil, agonisingly losing by a point to eventual champions South Africa. Dupont was instrumental as France bounced back to lift the 2025 Six Nations trophy.

The Martian "I really think he comes from another planet. He is our X-factor," waxed international teammate Cyril Baille.

Position	Scrum-half
Country	France
Test span	2017-
Test caps	59
Test points	75 (15T)

12
GUINNESS SIX NATIONS

RUGBY LEGENDS

LOOSEHEAD PROPS

Rugby is a game for all shapes and sizes, and in moving on to the forwards we start with players who can look short and squat and yet do a magnificent job for their team. Naturally, both props must be expert scrummagers, lift in the lineout, make their tackles, and hit rucks and mauls until they drop. The loosehead, however, scrummaging as he is against one player not two, is expected to do more around the field – think Cyril Baille and Ellis Genge. In the scrum, the loosehead tries to stay upright and help his hooker get a clean strike of the ball – easier said than done when a behemoth of a tighthead is bearing down on you.

11

GETHIN JENKINS

MAJOR TEAMS: Pontypridd, Celtic Warriors, Cardiff, Toulon

Many of the compliments directed towards Gethin Jenkins seem to come with a caveat. Former Wales assistant coach Rob Howley gives a taste of the trend.

"I won't say he has an outstanding personality. He is a grumpy so-and-so," explained the former scrum-half on the eve of Jenkins's 100th Test in March 2014. "But when I look back on my coaching career, I will be happy that I coached one of the best front-rowers that has played."

Gareth Rogers came up through the youth ranks at Pontypridd alongside the man known as 'Melon' and offered a similar sentiment that same year. "Sixteen years after we first met, I'm still finding it hard to believe that the burger-eating, cider-swilling monster I used to pack down with is Wales' record cap-holder," Rogers said.

The praise may be laced with humour. However, in rugby terms, Jenkins is truly revered. Having made his Wales debut against Romania in 2002, he featured at the 2003 World Cup and was an integral cog of the 2005 Grand Slam.

Charging down Ronan O'Gara before kicking ahead and scoring after a 40m sprint, he sent the Millennium Stadium into raptures and set up a 32-20 win over Ireland.

Mobility and awareness, as well as effective industry at the breakdown, characterised his contributions, and two more Six Nations clean sweeps arrived in 2008 and 2012. He made three Test starts on the 2005 Lions tour of New Zealand and was a standout of the 2009 voyage to South Africa before a fractured eye socket in the second Test ended his trip.

Jenkins captained his country as they thrashed England 30-3 to take the 2013 Six Nations and usurped fly-half Stephen Jones as the most-capped Welshman 12 months later. Nearly a decade on, only Alun Wyn Jones among his compatriots has eclipsed Jenkins's 129 Welsh caps.

In terms of domestic competition, Cardiff gave the prop his all-important breakthrough and though he signed for Toulon for two seasons – winning the 2013 Heineken Cup – Jenkins returned home after just one year on the French Riviera. He joined Wayne Pivac's staff in 2020 and currently coaches the Wales defence.

Position	Loosehead prop
Country	Wales
Test span	2002-16
Wales caps	129 (93 starts)
Lions caps	5 (5 starts)
Test points	20 (4T)

Gethin through Jenkins works some space versus Sharks on the 2009 Lions tour

WILSON WHINERAY

MAJOR TEAMS: Canterbury, Waikato, Auckland

Sir Wilson Whineray was that rugby rarity – a loosehead who had scrummaging maturity beyond his years.

The New Zealander's star shone brightly from the day he made his Test debut against Australia in 1957 aged 21, and it never dimmed in a career that spanned nine years. The last eight of these, moreover, were as skipper in 30 Internationals – a world record for Test captaincy that lasted nearly 20 years until beaten by the Frenchman Jean-Pierre Rives.

In open play, Whineray showed a range of deft touches, the legacy of his earlier days in a variety of positions in and behind the scrum. He had soft hands, sold convincing dummies and was adept at the long-lost art of dribbling.

His awkward packing technique caused front-row opponents problems. The most highly acclaimed tighthead of the era was

'Wil' power Brushing France aside

Springbok Piet du Toit, and their battles in South Africa in 1960 were titanic. Though the All Blacks narrowly lost the series, the Kiwi was the only loosehead of his time to neutralise the havoc for which du Toit was famed.

Whineray's captaincy style was autocratic, but New Zealand lost only five Tests while he was at the helm. The veteran critic Terry McLean unhesitatingly named him "New Zealand's greatest captain", while Colin Meads, an exact contemporary, spoke for a talented generation of All Blacks when he said, "As a captain he inspired fierce loyalty." High praise indeed from one who might easily have had his own designs on the leadership.

Note, too, the day in 1964 when Whineray's All Blacks skittled the Barbarians 36-3 in the traditional tour finale at Cardiff. As the skipper dummied and sidestepped to the posts to complete the try-scoring, an admiring full house was roused to sing *For He's A Jolly Good Fellow*. It was a fitting tribute to a great player and captain.

Position	Loosehead prop
Country	New Zealand
Test span	1957-65
Test caps	32 (32 starts)
Test points	6 (2T)

IAN MCLAUCHLAN

Winning blend McLauchlan had technique and tenacity

MAJOR TEAMS: Jordanhill, Glasgow

At only a shade over 5ft 8in, Ian McLauchlan was initially deemed too small by some to excel in international rugby. How the Scot enjoyed proving them wrong.

The man known around the globe as 'Mighty Mouse' was one of only five men to play in all eight Lions Tests in the glory years of the early 1970s, and it was the Ayrshire-born loosehead who kick-started the whole jamboree by charging down Alan Sutherland's attempted clearance to score early in the 1971 first Test in Dunedin.

It was the only Test try McLauchlan ever scored, but he brought so much else to the party. As a scrummager, he played havoc with the big New Zealand props, conceding 4st and 5in to Test rival Jazz Muller (who was so strong that he used a lawnmower to trim his garden hedge).

By bending his opponent and putting pressure on his neck, McLauchlan made New Zealand pay for underestimating the specialist nature of the prop position. Tight binding and low scrummaging negated the All Blacks' weight advantage, and the result was a Lions set-piece that laid the foundation for victory.

McLauchlan was also a force in the loose – Jim Telfer used to reckon he'd step on his own granny to get the ball – and he's irked to this day by suggestions that he only got his Lions place because of injury to the 'first choice' Ray McLoughlin.

Playing alongside Bobby Windsor and Fran Cotton in South Africa, McLauchlan was part of one of the all-time great front rows and he played 13 games on tour, captaining the Lions against Southern Universities.

A long-time PE teacher, McLauchlan also led Scotland 19 times, a record until being overtaken by David Sole.

After bowing out at the top level at the age of 37, he had a successful career in rugby administration that included the SRU presidency from 2010-12. He's now retired and lives on Islay.

Position	Loosehead prop
Country	Scotland
Test span	1969-79
Scotland caps	43 (43 starts)
Lions caps	8 (8 starts)
Test points	3 (1T)

CIAN HEALY

MAJOR TEAMS: Leinster

A member of the exclusive club of active players who began their international careers back in the 2000s, the seemingly indestructible front rower is a study in durability and no player in any position has made more appearances for either Ireland or Leinster than the evergreen veteran. Healy's enviable collection of winner's medals reflects his incredible length of service for both country and province.

The prop debuted in the 20-20 draw with Australia at Croke Park in 2009. He was first choice loosehead for the Six Nations the following year and in 2013 he earned selection for the Lions tour of Australia, although he did not feature in any of the three Tests Down Under.

That disappointment, however, was quickly forgotten in 2014, as Ireland lifted the Championship trophy for the second time in the Six Nations era. They defended their title 12 months later, but it was in the 2018 edition of the tournament that Healy etched his name into Irish rugby folklore as the team sealed a famous Grand Slam, the Leinster star playing in all five of their victorious outings.

A technically gifted front rower rather than one who relies on brute force, Healy's acceleration and deft hands make equally comfortable in the loose as the scrum. He made two appearances in green in 2023, as Ireland secured another coveted Grand Slam, and in late 2024 he set a new national record with his 134 Test for his country, against the Wallabies in Dublin, surpassing the previous milestone set by former team-mate Brian O'Driscoll. Three months later he surpassed O'Driscoll's appearance record for Ireland in the Six Nations.

No player has featured in more European Rugby Championship Cup matches than Healy. He set the record in May 2024 against Northampton, his 111th appearance in the tournament to move him ahead of Ronan O'Gara, and over the course of his remarkable provincial career with Leinster he has lifted the most prestigious trophy in European club rugby four times.

The prop has proved equally long-lived on United Rugby Championship duty. His 281st game in the competition in September 2024 against the Dragons established a new Leinster cap record and he has won the URC no less than seven times since collecting his first winner's medal in 2008.

After a remarkable 137 Test appearances, Healy's Ireland career came to an end in the 2025 Six Nations with the front rower marking the emotional occasion with a try against France at the Aviva.

Position	Loosehead prop
Country	Ireland
Test span	2009–25
Test caps	137
Test points	65 (13T)

Emerald Isle icon No one has played more Tests for Ireland than the Leinster front row legend

MAJOR TEAMS: Saracens, Harlequins

Jason Leonard came over as the cheeky chappie who hadn't a care in the world, but beneath the cheerful surface lay a steely determination to set consistently high standards. The physical and mental preparations he put into match days were so focused that his tackle count was always remarkably high for a prop, while he conceded very few penalties.

Born in Barking and educated at the university of hard knocks, Leonard joined his local club, where his strength attracted the attention of London's top-flight outfits. He made his first-class

JASON LEONARD

English musketeer Leonard has always shown an 'all for one' devotion to the team cause

debut for Saracens as a teenager and at 21 – the youngest prop to play for England for 27 years – debuted against Argentina in Buenos Aires. Brian Moore, England's hooker that day, praised the loosehead's solid and reliable qualities.

Leonard transferred to Harlequins on his return but in 1992 underwent a delicate neck operation to correct a career-threatening injury. Through his dedication to training and fitness, he overcame that setback to stay at the top of his game throughout a decade that saw demands on leading players change beyond recognition as rugby entered its professional era.

Leonard made three Lions tours, crossing the front row to deputise on the starboard side for the 1993 series in New Zealand. Ian McGeechan regards him as the ultimate Lion because of his selfless devotion to the team cause ahead of any personal ambitions. When Leonard failed to make the 1997 Lions Test side, McGeechan said: "It must have been a crushing disappointment, yet he spent time with Paul Wallace, putting everything into making him ready."

Position	Loosehead prop
Country	England
Test span	1990-2004
England caps	114 (102 starts)
Lions caps	5 (2 starts)
Test points	5 (1T)

It was typical of a player who was a fixture in the England side for 14 years. He featured in four Grand Slams, was a losing finalist against Australia in the 1991 World Cup and survived to enjoy revenge in 2003 when England won the trophy.

He became the first British player to reach 100 caps and retired in 2004 as England's most-capped player, an honour he still held going into the 2022 Six Nations. A former RFU president, he was appointed Lions chairman in 2019. His record-breaking feats prompted the former England and Lions stalwart Fran Cotton to baptise Leonard "English rugby's Don Bradman". There can be no better compliment than that.

FRAN COTTON

MAJOR TEAMS: Coventry, Sale

Brain and brawn combined to make Fran Cotton an all-time great. The son of a good rugby league player, young Fran took up union at grammar school, was capped by England while studying PE and maths at Loughborough University, and became a successful businessman and rugby administrator later in life.

His 6ft 2in frame helped him become an outstanding prop who could play on either side of the scrum. He had a hard edge, and after he punched his fellow Lion and tighthead rival Sandy Carmichael at public training on the 1974 tour to South Africa, he earned the Test spot and played a key role alongside Bobby Windsor and Ian McLauchlan for the unbeaten tourists.

Windsor said: "Frannie was massive on that Lions tour, like a great English oak."

In fact, the man from Wigan never lost a match in South Africa, playing there with England in 1972 and returning with the Lions in 1980, when he sadly had to head home after four appearances because of a heart condition.

Cotton's versatility meant he played loosehead in England's Grand Slam team of 1980 and on the 1977 Lions tour to New Zealand, when he was part of a pack so dominant that the All Blacks resorted to three-man scrums in a bid to get the ball straight out. It was on that trip that photographer Colin Elsey snapped the iconic 'mud man' picture of Cotton, his face caked in mud, his eyes gleaming through.

Cotton captained England three times and even led them in the World Cup Sevens in 1973. His career ended with a leg injury in 1981 and six years later he set up the Cotton Traders clothing company with team-mate Steve Smith.

Cotton was banned for a decade by the RFU for earning money from writing a book but was welcomed back in time to manage the 1997 Lions tour to South Africa. His success as a Lions player, understanding of the Springbok mentality and attention to detail meant he played a key role as the Lions upset the odds.

Position	Loosehead prop
Country	England
Test span	1971-81
England caps	31 (31 starts)
Lions caps	7 (7 starts)
Test points	4 (1T)

Fran-mountain Cotton took no prisoners

OS DU RANDT

MAJOR TEAMS: Free State Cheetahs

Os du Randt thought his time in Test rugby was finished after South Africa's 1999 tour to Europe, but little did he know that eight years later he would become the first Bok to win two global titles.

After being the starting loosehead in the 1995 triumph (at just 22), du Randt played in the 1999 tournament before suffering a spate of injuries that forced him to retire at the age of 28, with 39 caps.

Then the phone rang and it was his old mate – and former Springbok flanker – Rassie Erasmus on the end of the line, who asked him to turn out for Free State. One thing led to another and in 2004 du Randt was recalled to the Springboks by then national coach Jake White.

It was a masterstroke from White, who admitted there was more to it than just wanting to reinstate an old-fashioned loosehead prop to the Test team. White also wanted a man who was burning from being dropped in 1999 and had never had the chance to fight for his place, someone who could tell his group of players just how lucky they were to be pulling on the Springbok jersey.

In 2006 the South Africans arrived in Sydney on the back of a 35-17 thrashing by the All Blacks in Wellington and the camp was not a happy one. Du Randt, usually the archetypal strong and silent type, addressed the team and the rejuvenated Boks were only beaten 20-18 thanks to a conversion of a Mat Rogers try at the death. Du Randt, who had 67 caps by then, wept in the dressing room and was too upset to join the post-match meeting. But his message hit home with the younger members of the squad – a year later they became World Cup winners for the first time while du Randt wrapped his hands around his second World Cup winner's medal.

Position	Loosehead prop
Country	South Africa
Test span	1994-2007
Test caps	80 (75 starts)
Test points	25 (5T)

Mine's a double Du Randt is one of only two South Africans to win the Rugby World Cup twice

SYD MILLAR

Solid Syd Nine Lions Tests and coach of the Invincibles

MAJOR TEAMS: Ballymena, Ulster

To a younger audience, Syd Millar will be more familiar as an elder statesman of rugby administration, including a four-year stint as World Rugby chairman (from 2003 to 2007). Yet to those longer in the tooth, he was a hard-nosed prop from Country Antrim who played his club rugby with Ballymena and Ulster.

Despite being built like a brick outhouse, Millar started his career as an outside-half and was more than capable of stepping away from the coal face and playing a handling game. A highly technical prop, he prided himself on the set-piece and could play on either side of the scrum. Although tighthead was said to be his preference, he packed down at loosehead in both the 1959 and 1962 Lions series, and it's in that capacity that he makes our list.

Called up for Ireland in 1958, Millar won the first of his 37 caps against France in Colombes. He showed the tenacity that served him well in later years when, after being overlooked for nearly four years, he reclaimed his Ireland shirt, making a final 14 appearances before bowing out in 1970.

Millar went on to carve a reputation as a Lions talisman and he holds the distinction of being involved in more tours than his great friend Willie John McBride. Millar was involved in nine tours, playing in three, where he started in nine Tests.

He then coached the 1974 'Invincibles' to glory in South Africa and was chairman on the 2001 tour to Australia.

Position	Loosehead prop
Country	Ireland
Test span	1958-70
Ireland caps	37 (37 starts)
Lions caps	9 (9 starts)
Test points	0

TENDAI MTAWARIRA

Beast unleashed Mtawarira troubles the English in 2018

MAJOR TEAMS: Sharks

You always knew when Tendai Mtawarira was on the charge for the Sharks or the Springboks. When the 115kg prop dropped his shoulder, the crowd would growl "Beaaaast!" Mtawarira acquired his 'Beast' nickname at primary school in Harare – "I was a big, chubby fellow" he says – and it was to prove a fitting moniker during an 11-year Test career that saw him chew up many an opponent.

Two of his finest hours came ten years apart. In the first Lions Test of 2009, he earned a succession of scrum penalties against Phil Vickery to take the match away from the tourists in Durban. Fast-forward to Japan 2019 and he was at it again, this time outfoxing Dan Cole in the World Cup final as South Africa claimed the trophy for the third time.

Mtawarira retired soon afterwards, his 117 appearances putting him third on the Springboks' caps list behind Victor Matfield and Bryan Habana. He also played a record 159 Super Rugby games for the Sharks.

World Cup-winning coach Rassie Erasmus hailed Mtawarira's contribution to Springbok rugby as "enormous" and part of the player's legacy is aspirational. Growing up in Zimbabwe, he dreamt of playing in goal for Man Utd but changed tack after being introduced to rugby aged ten. He was spotted by Sharks' scouts while playing for Zimbabwe U18 in a tournament in South Africa and the franchise not only signed him up but moulded the then No 8 into a fearsome loosehead prop.

His strength is legendary and was highlighted by a remarkable moment in 2012 when Sharks lock Anton Bresler seemed sure to crash to the floor when trying to catch a kick-off, only for Mtawarira to hold him up by his shorts as he dangled behind the prop's back.

"Because of his achievements, a lot of black Zim and South African kids have belief it can be done," says a former team-mate Kisset Chirengende. "He was a trailblazer."

Position	Loosehead prop
Country	South Africa
Test span	2008-19
Test caps	117 (102 starts)
Test points	10 (2T)

TOM SMITH

Hands off Smith tries to evade the USA at the 2003 World Cup

MAJOR TEAMS: Watsonians, Dundee, Glasgow, Brive, Northampton

Size doesn't matter – as Tom Smith will testify. Despite a lack of size or experience, the Scot rocketed to prominence in 1997 after being picked for the Lions tour of South Africa. Far from a shoo-in for selection, he had played only three Tests for his country before he was selected by Ian McGeechan to go on the hallowed trip.

Once he was there, his strength in the scrum and his mobility stood him apart from other props; he offered a lot of power in a smaller package than most. He also did this with no boasting; Smith was as softly spoken and modest as players come.

If you think at 5ft 10in and 16st he sounds tiny for a modern prop, you will be shocked to hear he also played at No 8 for Scottish Schools. He always had ball skills – at age-grade level his coach, former Scotland lock Alastair McHarg, once yelled at him, "That's a one on your back, not a ten!"

It was Smith's pluck that made him stand out. He played six consecutive Lions Tests from 1997 to 2001. He captained Scotland for a brief period in 2001 and played in two World Cups, in 1999 and 2003. He was never once on the bench.

Smith was also a pivotal player for Northampton between 2001 and 2009, having previously played with Brive in France. Winning a Powergen Cup was big for Saints but Smith never made a fuss about it. He never made a fuss about anything.

This is all the more impressive when you realise that Smith suffered from epilepsy for his entire playing career. It never held him back. He once played a Calcutta Cup match after having a seizure that same day. And in 2019 he was diagnosed with colon cancer.

Setbacks, even those of such a serious nature, never faze him. He has always made the most of what he has and succeeded time and time again.

Position	Loosehead prop
Country	Scotland
Test span	1997-2005
Scotland caps	61 (61 starts)
Lions caps	6 (6 starts)
Test points	30 (6T)

RUGBY LEGENDS

HOOKERS

All the great hookers have caused damage in the loose – yet not at the expense of the set-piece basics that constitute the core part of their role. Ideally, the No 2 will scrummage as effectively as a prop, throw into lineouts with the precision of a surgeon's scalpel, and serve as a fourth loose forward in open play. Some will win regular turnovers at the breakdown, others carry and offload like a No 8. If you can also get on the score-sheet occasionally – England's Jamie Blamire bagged six tries in his first five Tests – then you have the complete package.

BOBBY WINDSOR

Uncompromising Windsor made for a terrifying opponent

MAJOR TEAMS: Brynglas, Cross Keys, Cardiff, Pontypool

He says he was always hungry as a kid and Bobby Windsor played his rugby with that same ferocious appetite for Wales and the Lions during a golden age for both teams.

At 16st-plus, he was built like a prop at a time of light hookers, and on the 1974 Lions tour he proved he was one of the great scrummaging front-rowers. The Lions would take the Springboks so low in the scrum that Windsor would sometimes hook with his head before driving over them, there being no law then about keeping shoulders above the hips.

As able to take a punch as deliver one, hence his 'Iron Duke' nickname, Windsor was made for that tour because of his love of the fight. Former Wales captain Eddie Butler calls him the best he ever played with. "Some hookers are good at some parts of their trade and not so good at others. Bobby was a master of them all," Butler said. "He was also vicious, the most cold-hearted brute you would never wish to see standing over you at a ruck."

At school at Newport, Windsor scored 56 goals in a soccer season, and he took that skill and pace with him into rugby, scoring a try on his Wales debut against Australia in his breakthrough campaign of 1973-74.

Over the next five-and-a-half years, he won 28 successive Welsh caps and became a double Lion and double Grand Slammer.

His club feats were no less notable, Windsor packing down with Charlie Faulkner and Graham Price in the famous 'Viet Gwent' Pontypool front row that shared many a triumph on the Test stage. The trio played together for Wales 19 times and for the Lions in Fiji on 16 August 1977 (the day Elvis died).

Advised to retire in 1980 because of a back injury, Windsor continued to play on for another seven years. Legendary coach Ray Prosser hailed him as the only tight forward he saw who could change the course of a game. Wales have not seen the like of him again.

Position	Hooker
Country	Wales
Test span	1973-79
Wales caps	28 (28 starts)
Lions caps	5 (5 starts)
Test points	4 (1T)

SEAN FITZPATRICK

MAJOR TEAMS: Auckland, Blues

As the son of an All Black, Sean Fitzpatrick had genetics on his side. But it took some epiphanic moments to ensure that he went the distance in a career that brought him 92 caps, 51 of them as captain, and an astounding 82% win rate.

Two in particular stand out. On tour for Auckland in 1983, the youngster was taken to task by lock Andy Haden for his lineout throwing in training. "He told me he wasn't going to waste his time and made me go and fetch another hooker," says Fitzpatrick, who then spent six months perfecting his art.

Then, in 1991, with 40-odd caps under his belt, Fitzpatrick was jolted from a sense of complacency by seeing a newspaper article hailing Aussie rival Phil Kearns as the best hooker in the world. Fitzpatrick changed his attitude and went on to become an indestructible presence and captain of one of the best teams in sporting history. The World Cup cruelly eluded the All Blacks in South Africa in 1995, but they returned the next year to become the first New Zealand side to win a series in the Rainbow Nation.

Fitzpatrick's mantra was 'be the best you can be', and to his remorseless drive and refusal to yield to injuries – he started all but the last of his 92 Test appearances, giving way to Norm Hewitt in 1997 because of a chronic knee condition – he added a dollop of luck.

An injury to Andy Dalton opened the door for Fitzpatrick to play in the 1987 World Cup-winning XV, while his selection as captain in 1992 followed an injury to Laurie Main's first-choice skipper Mike Brewer in the final trial.

If the fates smiled on him, Fitzpatrick has repeatedly seized the day, even emigrating to London in 2003 because there were more opportunities there to forge a career in media punditry, speaking engagements and corporate hospitality.

Position	Hooker
Country	New Zealand
Test span	1986-97
Test caps	92 (91 starts)
Test points	55 (12T)

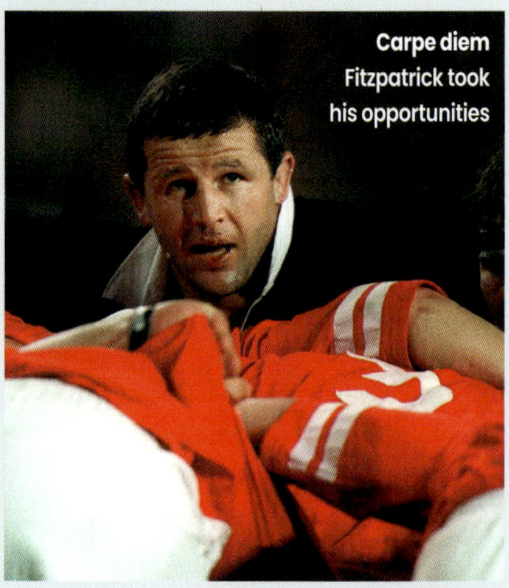

Carpe diem Fitzpatrick took his opportunities

BISMARCK DU PLESSIS

Shove it! Du Plessis set the bar for modern hookers

MAJOR TEAMS: Free State Cheetahs, Natal, Sharks, Montpellier, Bulls

Stuck behind the sizeable figure of skipper John Smit, Bismarck du Plessis only accrued two starts in the first 14 Tests of his Springbok career. While those cameos involved an appearance in the 2007 World Cup final triumph against England, a year of frustration evidently fuelled a fire of ambition.

When controversial Springbok head coach Peter de Villiers decided to shift Smit to tighthead in 2008, it was partly because du Plessis had outgrown his role as an impact replacement.

Dynamic and abrasive, and with exceptional breakdown nous, the God-fearing farmer's boy from Bethlehem in the Free State – who is also a qualified insurance broker – set about establishing himself as one of the most respected hookers on the planet.

The 2009 series against the Lions offered an impressive foundation, du Plessis playing all 160 minutes of the first two Tests and helping to carve out an unassailable 2-0 lead thanks to a pair of menacing, obdurate performances.

A 32-29 victory in Hamilton in 2009 then completed a hat-trick of wins over the All Blacks and added that season's Tri-Nations title for the Springboks.

One of the best jacklers in the global game, du Plessis has had elder brother Jannie for support most of the way. The pair debuted for South Africa in the same game against the Wallabies in 2007 and shared seven years together at the Sharks as well. In 2015 they left Durban for Montpellier, from where Bismarck returned home last year, joining the Bulls.

In later times, Adriaan Strauss emerged as another international rival, and red-mist moments brought du Plessis bans for alleged eye-gouging and kicking during his otherwise illustrious career.

According to former Sharks coach Gary Gold, however, du Plessis's overall reputation remains unblemished.

"Bismarck is comfortably the best hooker in the world," Gold, now the USA head coach, once said. "Nobody else can hold a flame to him. His throwing is outstanding, his scrummaging huge and his work-rate around the park immense."

Position	Hooker
Country	South Africa
Test span	2007-15
Test caps	79 (50 starts)
Test points	55 (11T)

PETER WHEELER

Wheel deal Wheeler moves the ball against France in 1978

MAJOR TEAMS: Leicester Tigers

Becoming chief executive at Leicester Tigers in 1996 and moving to a director position 14 years later, Wheeler is known to the younger generation as an administrative heavyweight. Following the advent of professionalism, this former RFU president helped uphold the traditions of a hugely proud club while maintaining a steady stream of trophies. Yet for slightly older aficionados, his on-field prowess and list of honours were even more impressive.

Tough and technically proficient, Wheeler was a hooker who was rarely bettered in the tight exchanges. However, the extracurricular activity around the pitch truly set him apart.

Captaining Leicester to three consecutive John Player Cups between 1979 and 1981, he was integral to an innovative, expansive style of play. "We didn't have the biggest pack of forwards at the time," he would say on reflection two decades later. "But we were playing an open, attacking style of rugby that inspired people. We scored a lot of tries from all over the place."

Having made his first-team bow in 1969, Wheeler finished on 349 appearances for the Tigers. His ability was not consigned to domestic duty, though – far from it.

By the time he met France on his Test debut in 1975, Wheeler had already toured the Far East with England and been on standby for the 1974 Lions trip to South Africa.

Some outstanding form for his country

Position	Hooker
Country	England
Test span	1975-84
England caps	48 (48 starts)
Lions caps	7 (7 starts)
Test points	0

– he took four strikes against the head in a 23-6 defeat of Australia in 1976 – earned him a spot in the 1977 British & Irish Lions squad, and the then 28-year-old usurped Welshman Bobby Windsor to face the All Blacks three times.

Only poor back play prevented the Lions from taking the series, but Wheeler never let defeat deter him. Instead, he became the heartbeat of Bill Beaumont's dominant pack three years later in South Africa, when a 17-13 victory at Loftus Versfeld allowed the tourists to end the season on a high.

KEITH WOOD

MAJOR TEAMS: Garryowen, Harlequins, Munster

Keith Wood never took a backward step, on or off the field. A combative hooker with an intensity that often bordered on lunacy – who can forget him maniacally haring after a kick upfield on the 1997 Lions tour? – he encapsulated the clichéd phrase 'force of nature'.

Brought up in County Clare, where he spent his youth hurling, his rugby pedigree was never in question after his father Gordon packed down for Ireland on 29 occasions. He made his debut at 21 against the Wallabies in 1994 and went on to captain Ireland in 36 Tests.

Wood excelled at the set-piece, finding his jumper routinely, yet what set him apart from his peers was his attacking ability. The man nicknamed 'Uncle Fester' for his distinctive bald head crossed the try-line 15 times in his 58 Tests – a world record for a hooker until being eclipsed by USA's Joe Taufete'e in 2019. The memory of the 17st Wood throwing in and then tearing around the corner to take the ball off the jumper to drive into the opposition defence is a sight few opponents will miss.

Wood led Ireland into the last of his three World Cups. His 1999 campaign included a four-try haul against the USA, while he bowed out against France in the 2003 quarter-finals. "The heart is willing, the head is willing, but the body has had enough," he said.

Wood was also to make a name for himself as a Lion, playing in five Tests. He was one of the standout players in both 1997 and 2001, winning the inaugural World Player of the Year award in the latter year.

Domestically, Wood spent the majority of his pro career with Harlequins, save for a year with Munster when he led them to the Heineken Cup final in 2000, giving them a belief they could conquer Europe.

After retiring, Wood founded W2 Consulting, specialists in business and leadership support.

Position	Hooker
Country	Ireland
Test span	1994-2003
Ireland caps	58 (55 starts)
Lions caps	5 (5 starts)
Test points	75 (15T)

Class is permanent Wood followed his father into he Irish shirt, winning the first World Player of the Year award

JOHN SMIT

MAJOR TEAMS: Sharks, Clermont, Saracens

An uncomplicated but hugely impactful hooker, Smit's record-breaking reign as South Africa captain was the catalyst for a golden era for the Springboks in which they lifted the World Cup for a second time in their history, claimed the Tri Nations title and sealed a series victory over the Lions, avenging their painful loss to the tourists 12 years earlier.

First capped against Canada in East London in 2000, Smit set a national record between October 2003 and June 2007 with 46 consecutive Test appearances. He was made captain in 2004 and three years later led from the front as the Springboks were crowned world champions after despatching England 15-6 in the final in the Stade de France.

Position	Hooker
Country	South Africa
Test span	2000–2011
Test caps	111
Test points	40 (8T)

Rugby World Cup glory was followed in 2009 with a cathartic success against the Lions. South Africa had lost 2-1 in 1997, the first post-apartheid series against the tourists, but under Smit's leadership the scoreline was reversed in 2009. He scored the opening try in the first Test triumph in Durban. There was precious little time for celebrations, however, with the Springboks in Tri Nations action against New Zealand only three weeks after the series, and after five wins from six in the tournament, including three famous victories over the All Blacks, they were kings of the southern hemisphere.

During the tournament Smit won his 60th cap as skipper in the 31-19 win over the Kiwis in Durban, a new Test rugby record which eclipsed the previous mark jointly held by Australia's George Gregan and England's Will Carling.

His international retirement came after

the 2011 Rugby World Cup. Thirteen of his 111 caps, a then Springbok record, came at prop rather than hooker. In total he led his country in his own inimitable, understated style in 83 matches, another world record until it was eventually surpassed by Brian O'Driscoll, Sergio Parisse and Richie McCaw.

Domestically, the front rower spent his entire Super Rugby career with the Sharks, captaining the side for seven seasons, before heading north to Europe to play for Clermont in the Top 14 and then Saracens in the English Premiership.

RAPHAËL IBAÑEZ

MAJOR TEAMS: Dax, Perpignan, Castres, Saracens, Wasps

Once the world's most-capped hooker, Raphaël Ibañez lifted trophies at domestic, European and international level and was a popular and respected player and leader.

He took over the France captaincy at the start of 1998 on just his third Test start and led les Bleus to a Grand Slam that year. Three more Six Nations titles followed, while Ibañez also played in three World Cups, captaining his country at the 1999 and 2007 events.

He concedes that he had a confidence crisis after his first World Cup when new coach Bernard Laporte, seeking cool-headed discipline in place of hot-headed passion, suggested Ibañez wasn't the type of hooker he wanted.

Position	Hooker
Country	France
Test span	1996-2007
Test caps	98 (75 starts)
Test points	40 (8T)

Ibañez got the message, reassessing his mental approach and sharpening up in every technical area, as well as adding weight without any loss of mobility. In short, he became an even better player, and if he hadn't retired from Test rugby after the 2003 World Cup – only to return in 2005 – he would have exceeded a century of France caps. Only Pelous (111) and Philippe Sella (118) have more than him.

Born in Dax in the Basques region in 1973, Ibañez grew up around bull fighting and rugby, as his father Jacques played hooker for the hometown club. Ibañez played for Dax from 1991-98, then had spells at Perpignan and Castres before crossing the Channel to join Saracens after the 2003 World Cup.

In 2005 Ian McGeechan lured him to Wasps and Ibañez shared in some of their greatest triumphs. There was none better than the 2007 Heineken Cup final, when Ibañez scored one try and made another through two brilliant lineout moves against Leicester. He was named club captain but a series of concussions that autumn

Tears of joy Ibañez brought passion to the field

prompted Ibañez to retire in 2009.

Having done some coaching with Wasps Academy while he was still playing, Ibañez made the move into management and took up the reins at Bordeaux-Begles in 2012.

Now 49, he was hotly tipped to succeed Philippe Saint-André as France coach in 2015 but is now team manager working with head coach Fabien Galthié.

COLIN DEANS

Scottish dynamo
Deans races down the wing against France

MAJOR TEAMS: Hawick

He won a Grand Slam with Scotland in 1984, led them to the first World Cup and received an MBE after retiring as his country's most-capped player in 1987. Yes, Colin Deans had much to celebrate in his career, but he was denied the chance to add a hatful of Lions caps to his memorabilia collection because the captain of the 1983 squad was his rival for the No 2 shirt, Ireland's Ciaran Fitzgerald.

It seems almost everyone, except tour manager Willie John McBride and Fitzgerald himself, thought Deans should have played the four Tests against the All Blacks, but he had to be content playing seven non-capping matches while the Test side was whitewashed 4-0. Some redemption came when, three years later, he led the Lions in a one-off match against a Rest of the World XV in Cardiff to mark the IRB's (now World Rugby) centenary. Bill McLaren was among those who coached Deans when he was a Hawick schoolboy, while Eddie Jones has declared the brilliant Borderer as his hero. Standing 5ft 10in tall but light in stature by current standards, Deans was the first of a new breed of mobile hookers who played like an extra back-row – although he was still famed for his accurate lineout throwing and his swift striking at scrum time.

Position	Hooker
Country	Scotland
Test span	1978-87
Test caps	52 (52 starts)
Test points	10 (2T)

He won his first cap in 1978 aged 22, and had to wait until his 11th Test to get a win, although Deans himself says he doesn't count that victory over France in February 1980 because he came off injured.

Happier days followed as Deans helped Scotland draw 25-25 with New Zealand in November 1983 – the last time they avoided defeat by the All Blacks – and then claim the Grand Slam in 1984.

By 1986 he was Scotland captain and the following year he led them to the World Cup, winning his final cap in the quarter-final defeat by New Zealand.

Seeing an opportunity in the lamination market place, he started his own company, Profoil, in 1996. Deans is a Northampton Saints fan and was on the coaching staff at the club from 1995-2001.

MARIO LEDESMA

Position	Hooker
Country	Argentina
Test span	1996-2011
Test caps	84 (67 starts)
Test points	15 (3T)

MAJOR TEAMS: Curupatyi, Narbonne, Castres, Clermont Auvergne

Former Wallabies prop Sekope Kepu might seem an odd choice to present a shrewd depiction of Mario Ledesma's character, not least because he was only ten when the Argentinian made his Test debut against Uruguay in 1996. However, in describing the nature of Ledesma's set-piece sessions with the Waratahs – where the former Puma acted as a consultant coach under Michael Cheika – Kepu encapsulates the passion and enthusiasm that filled his mentor's blue-and-white jersey.

"At training we have one-minute scrums," Kepu said. "He's crawling in and out underneath us. We're thinking, 'Geez, if this comes down, you're crushed.' But that's the trust he's instilled in us."

You could argue that Ledesma's faith in the stability of an Australia scrum may be misplaced. But what was undeniable during the hooker's playing days was similarly unreserved commitment.

'Super Mario' earned his nickname with a remarkable World Cup record, playing in 18 matches at four tournaments from 1999. His career also took him to the Top 14 and he was a French title winner with Clermont in 2010. As Argentina's current head coach, he will be back in France for RWC 2023.

Spearheading a golden generation that catapulted Argentinian rugby into global consciousness, he was a relentless presence in the loose while fronting an extremely effective pack at both scrum and lineout.

One of many natural leaders in his generation – he captained the side against Japan on just his 15th cap – Ledesma was often seen with tears pouring down his cheeks during the national anthem.

In fact, such emotion became a hallmark of RWC 2007, where Argentina beat hosts France, Ireland and Scotland on their way to a stunning third-place finish. Four years later, a quarter-final defeat by New Zealand signalled Ledesma's exit. Among Pumas hookers, only Agustín Creevy has won more caps than Ledesma's 84-Test haul.

Making way for Creevy at Auckland's Eden Park, Ledesma began to cry. There was almost certainly a streak of sadness, but phenomenal pride too.

Dad done good Ledesma cradles his son after the Pumas' RWC 2007 win over Ireland

BRIAN MOORE

Toast of Twickenham
Moore raises a hip flask as fans savour the 1992 Grand Slam

MAJOR TEAMS: Nottingham, Harlequins, Richmond

A fierce competitiveness is part and parcel of being an elite athlete, but in Brian Moore rugby found a sportsman who took the trait to the nth degree. Moore once spent a week's worth of school breaks staring at a wall in punishment for not apologising for comments made in a games lesson that he felt were justified. That stubbornness was to stay with him during a career that brought him 63 starts as England hooker – a long-time national record until surpassed by Dylan Hartley.

Adopted as a baby, Moore grew up in Yorkshire and played in the backs before an injury led to him filling in at hooker in an U16 schools trial. He never looked back. Moore went through the ranks, captaining England B at the age of 23, and when hooker Graham Dawe was banned in the wake of the violent 1987 Five Nations match with Wales, Moore seized his chance.

He made his England debut in the ensuing Calcutta Cup match, gritting his teeth through the pain of a foot injury sustained in sprinting practice. Still troubled by the injury at the first World Cup, he took strong painkillers every day to get through the tournament and deny Dawe the opportunity to regain the shirt.

Moore's fiery intensity is renowned – hence his 'Pitbull' moniker – and he was one of the fittest players to wear the Red Rose. His sprint times over 30m and 60m were quicker than several England backs. One manic gym session, in which he vied furiously with Dawe, has passed into lore.

Yet he was also a nuts-and-bolts hooker, especially in the scrum, where, in tandem with Paul Rendall and Jeff Probyn, he took the French scrum so low that rival hooker Daniel Dubroca couldn't strike the ball.

Rugby World's Player of the Year in 1991, Moore found defeats hard to handle and he threw his RWC 1991 runners-up medal in the Thames in disgust. He won three Grand Slams yet felt it should have been five.

A qualified solicitor, Moore was often at loggerheads with the RFU over the amateur laws. His trenchant comments now enjoy a wide audience in his capacity as a media analyst, including coverage of the women's Six Nations for BBC Sport.

Position	Hooker
Country	England
Test span	1987–95
England caps	64 (63 starts)
Lions caps	5 (5 starts)
Test points	4 (1T)

RUGBY LEGENDS

TIGHTHEAD PROPS

The tighthead prop can command one of the biggest salaries in the pro game because of their importance in anchoring the scrum. As a No 3, you are generally bigger, stronger and more technical than a loosehead, because you are seeking to stay square and immovable while hemmed in by two opponents. Anyone accomplished at both roles is a pretty special player, but don't expect the adoration of spectators – this is not a glamorous role! Rather, it's made for those who relish a highly physical, one-to-one confrontation within the wider confines of a team game.

canterbury
IRFU

adidas
UAR
VISA

JEAN-PIERRE GARUET

Pack animal Garuet was a colossus in the French scrum

MAJOR TEAMS: Lourdes

Obstinate. It's the only way to describe Jean-Pierre Garuet's approach to the scrum. France adores the flat-backed, hairy brutes who relish tight exchanges and in Garuet they had a king amongst monsters.

Like so many fabled players, after some revision Garuet's general play has been reduced to one aspect: the set-piece. But from his 1983 Test debut against Australia the potato farmer was so good at it.

Technically superb and indefatigable whenever the restart was needed, Garuet earned plaudits from so many of his adversaries. After every tour the opposition would remark on how he could almost single-handedly tear a scrum apart, and he played a major role in guiding France to the inaugural World Cup final in 1987.

He was unapologetically tough, too. Trailblazer may be the wrong word but Garuet certainly is a man for a first, as no Frenchman had received a red card in a Test before he came along. In 1984 he made a play for Ireland flanker John O'Driscoll's eye. The prop was slammed with a three-month ban and brandished a "fool" by his own president, but he worked hard to repair his reputation.

That didn't mean backing down – in the infamous 'Battle of Nantes', it was Garuet who knocked Buck Shelford out cold when he flew into the New Zealander at a ruck.

He was not shy of afters, old Garuet, but perhaps this stems from a compelling loyalty. He'd fight to the death for his side, as evidenced by his club career: he only ever played for Lourdes, his home town, and played one last season for the side at 38, a year after France stopped picking him.

When the *Daily Mail* chose a Six Nations XV in 2015, Garuet was installed at No 3. "French packs have possessed some great props down the years," they opined, "but Garuet was arguably the greatest of the lot."

Position	Tighthead prop
Country	France
Test span	1983-90
Test caps	42 (41 starts)
Test points	0

OLO BROWN

MAJOR TEAMS: Ponsonby, Auckland

The foundation stone on which New Zealand's great pack of the 1990s was built, Olo Brown was one of the greatest props world rugby has seen, but also one of the game's most low-profile superstars as he shunned press conferences and interviews.

Born in Apia, Samoa, he emerged from Mount Albert Grammar School in Auckland with good enough academic results to become a chartered accountant and good enough rugby skills to oust Peter Fatialofa from the Auckland side in 1989, when Brown was only 21.

A year later, the Ponsonby prop was summoned from a New Zealand Development tour of Canada as injury cover for the All Blacks' tour of France, but he didn't earn his first Test cap until June 1992. Once he was in the side Brown proved unmovable in more ways than one and missed just a single Test in the next six years, when he was rested against Japan during the 1995 World Cup.

Position	Tighthead prop
Country	New Zealand
Test span	1992-98
Test caps	56 (56 starts)
Test points	20 (4T)

Alongside Sean Fitzpatrick and Steve McDowell, and later Craig Dowd, he anchored the scrum as they replicated their Auckland form on the Test stage. The All Blacks website pays this tribute, "He was the cornerstone of the pack. With his technique and straightness of back, he was rated by scrummaging experts as one of the finest props to play for New Zealand at any time. His provincial and Test team-mate, Sean Fitzpatrick, swore by his prowess and few scrums anchored by Brown were ever bettered."

Brown, who is related to former All Blacks captain Tana Umaga, finished on the winning side in 40 of his 56 Tests. His rich bounty included a series victory against the Lions in 1993 and nine wins out of 14 against both South Africa and Australia. He was the first All Blacks prop to reach 50 caps.

When rugby went pro, he continued his accountancy work but still played the first three seasons of Super Rugby with the Blues, winning the title in 1996 and 1997.

Brown's career was ended by a neck and back injury suffered against the Springboks in 1998. Typically, this media-shy giant never officially announced his retirement. "He was an awesome player, a truly brilliant scrummager," said Lawrence Dallaglio.

Immovable Brown was the first NZ prop to 50 caps

ADAM JONES

Hair apparent Jones derailed Australia's scrum during the 2013 Lions tour

MAJOR TEAMS: Neath, Ospreys, Cardiff, Harlequins

Adam Jones was christened 'Bomb' in a fond reference to 1990s American wrestler Adam Bomb, who sported similarly curly locks and an identical Christian name.

However, the moniker took on another dimension when Wales' longest-serving front-rower was at his peak. Destructive scrummaging rendered him a saboteur capable of obliterating the opposition.

Nowhere was this better demonstrated than over the first six months of 2013 prior to the introduction of new engagement laws.

On 16 March, England arrived at a raucous Millennium Stadium with designs on a Grand Slam. Runaway flanker Justin Tipuric created two headline-grabbing tries, but Jones dominated the tight exchanges to garner a succession of penalties. Amid an atmosphere heady with emotion, Stuart Lancaster's side were dismantled 30-3. They left the Six Nations trophy on the west of the Severn Bridge.

That summer, Australia's front row was comprehensively undone by a Lions scrum spearheaded by Jones in all three Tests. The successful series decider brought Bomb's international roll of honour to four Six Nations titles, including three Grand Slams, and five Lions caps – the first of which, as a second-half replacement at Durban in 2009, saw Springbok loosehead Tendai 'Beast' Mtawarira shackled after he had turned Phil Vickery inside out.

Four domestic crowns in 11 years at the Ospreys underlined Jones's class, though things weren't always straightforward. In the 2003 World Cup quarter-final against England, he lasted 27 minutes before being hauled off – a shock he later admitted forced him to confront early-career fitness issues.

After a decade saturated with silverware, Jones's 100th Test against South Africa in June 2014 brought a sad symmetry as Warren Gatland replaced him on the half-hour mark.

Exclusion from the 2015 Six Nations squad hastened his international retirement but this most affable of props began a new chapter at Harlequins, where he remains today as a highly respected scrum coach.

On announcing the signing, Conor O'Shea revealed that he had received a text from England's Joe Marler. The victim of Jones's formidable performance in Cardiff two years previously had simply written, "Glad he's on my side now."

Position	Tighthead prop
Country	Wales
Test span	2003-14
Wales caps	95 (84 starts)
Lions caps	5 (4 starts)
Test points	10 (2T)

MARTÍN SCELZO

Steely intent Scelzo on the hoof for the Pumas in 2010

MAJOR TEAMS: Northampton, Narbonne, Clermont Auvergne, Agen

Playing at tighthead prop is rarely, if ever, a case of rocking up to a big stage for the first time, packing down and blowing everyone away. More often, playing at No 3 means honing your craft and taking your beatings over time until you're the most resourceful and resilient scrummager.

It's with that spirit of endeavour that Martín Scelzo rose to renown. A Test player in 1996, any glamour in those early years of professionalism passed him by as he continued to graft away at the amateur Hindu club in a district of Buenos Aires.

It wasn't until after the 1999 World Cup that the tighthead was lured from his homeland, playing a part in Northampton Saints' Heineken Cup win at Twickenham in 2000. He was continuing to learn.

A frequent try-scorer in his early Test career, Scelzo had a number of team-mates to contend with during his time. Omar Hasan, Mauricio Reggiardo and later Juan Figallo all vied with Scelzo to be a starter. But the Pumas tighthead is not an easy role. So much onus is placed on the scrummage, and so much passion flows through the pack, that the exhaustion can go bone-deep. Scelzo kept picking himself up. By the time the 2007 World Cup rolled around, Scelzo was 31 and had learned things the hard way. Domestically he had played a major role in changing the identity of his club Clermont – to this day coach Vern Cotter calls him a "legend" for the work he did. Internationally, he was one-third of a terrifying front three next to Rodrigo Roncero and Mario Ledesma.

Sometimes people find their time in the world. For Scelzo it was that 2007 World Cup in France. He was magnificent in the set-piece and unforgiving in the loose.

After dominating for a few more years, he played in a fourth World Cup in New Zealand, having to send for new boots after accidentally only packing one pair – both for left feet. By then his best days were behind him, but for a brief window he was a true world master.

Position	Tighthead prop
Country	Argentina
Test span	1996–2011
Test caps	59 (33 starts)
Test points	50 (10T)

OWEN FRANKS

MAJOR TEAMS: Canterbury, Crusaders, Northampton Saints, Hurricanes, Toulouse

It takes a formidable athlete to cope with the abrasive challenges of playing in the front row at international level for any prolonged period of time. It is a famously unforgiving environment but one which Franks conquered for a decade, making him one of an extremely rare breed of props to have played more than 100 Tests for their country at the coal face.

The younger of the Franks brothers to represent New Zealand – Ben Franks won 47 caps – the tighthead made his international bow in 2009 against Italy and almost without interruption, provided the solidest of foundations for the All Black scrum for the next 10 years.

His remarkable durability was evidenced by his glittering World Cup career. He debuted in the 2011 edition of the tournament on home soil, starting in the dramatic but tense 8-7 win over the French in Auckland in the final. He was back in the trenches four years later at Twickenham as the Wallabies were swept aside 34-17 in the showpiece match. In total, Franks played in 13 of New Zealand's 14 matches over the two campaigns which yielded back-to-back global titles.

Tenacious and painfully impactful in defence, Franks holds the dubious distinction for the most caps in Test rugby without scoring a point, but it is no more than a distraction from his otherwise standout career. He joined the exclusive club of cap centurions in 2018 at Eden Park as New Zealand put the Wallabies to the sword and made his 108th and final appearance for the Kiwis the following year, again against Australia, in a resounding 47-26 Bledisloe Cup victory in Perth.

The tighthead was also a serial champion beyond the World Cup. He lifted the Tri Nations with New Zealand in 2010 and was a winner six further times, after the tournament had embraced Argentina and rebranded as the expanded Rugby Championship, while he also claimed a hat-trick of Super Rugby titles in Crusaders' colours between 2017 and 2019.

Position	Tighthead prop
Country	New Zealand
Test span	2009–2019
Test caps	108
Test points	0

IAIN MILNE

Incredible hulk Milne anchored the '84 Grand Slam pack

MAJOR TEAMS: Heriot's, Harlequins

In 2011, at a gala dinner in Paris, a mighty foe from bygone years was inducted into the French Hall of Fame. Iain Milne, the famous Bear of Scotland, was that man. To give you some idea of how significant that is, Milne's Test career overlapped with some of France's most vicious scrummaging beasts: Paparemborde, Dubroca, Garuet and Vaquerin all saw Milne in action. They all held him in very high regard – and they certainly punched him enough times to show that.

Milne received his nickname because he was a huge, immovable man, but he wasn't always that size. At school he was much smaller but time spent working on the docks once his education was over saw the Heriot's product develop incredible strength and bulk.

A leading light of Scotland's all-conquering 1984 Grand Slam side, the Edinburgh-born Milne was singled out for special praise by the great Jim Telfer that year, while his hooker Colin Deans later said: "He gave you the sure-fire feeling that the right-hand side of the scrum was going nowhere."

One of three brothers who all played for Scotland – David had a single cap at loosehead while Kenny was a hooker for Scotland and the Lions, and the three played a match together for the Barbarians – he also had undervalued ball skills.

Milne went on the 1983 Lions tour of New Zealand but, despite being in superb form, couldn't dislodge the great Graham Price. It was a pain he took with him into the 1984 Five Nations.

His power would not always go unrecognised. At that same dinner in 2011, former All Black Steve McDowell – the loosehead who faced Milne in the RWC 1987 quarter-finals and the opponent the Bear rated the highest – admitted that at the time the Kiwis felt Scotland were the best scrummagers on the planet.

As Milne was their anchor and key force, that is high praise indeed.

Position	Tighthead prop
Country	Scotland
Test span	1979-90
Test caps	44 (44 starts)
Test points	0

CARL HAYMAN

Diving exhibition Hayman scores against Portugal at the 2007 World Cup

MAJOR TEAMS: Otago, Highlanders, Newcastle Falcons, Toulon

Carl Hayman made his Test debut from the bench against Samoa at North Harbour in June 2001, the same game that also saw Marty Holah and Mark Ranby open their account. By virtue of alphabetical order, Hayman became the 1,000th All Black. In that regard, his legacy was secure from the off.

But while the hulking specimen from Opunake would only win a further 44 caps, his staggering power would smash the mould and live long in the memory.

Taller than the stereotypical tighthead at a relatively towering 6ft 4in, Hayman started out as a lock and a No 8.

His Super Rugby form for the Highlanders didn't translate into a consistent run of Test appearances until Graham Henry took the All Blacks reins in 2004. From Henry's first assignment – a 2-0 series win over world champions England – Hayman was entrenched in the No 3 jersey. He annihilated the French that November and, as a hugely effective lineout lifter, delivered a set-piece platform ranging between rock-solid and devastating.

Position	Tighthead prop
Country	New Zealand
Test span	2001-07
Test caps	45 (37 starts)
Test points	10 (2T)

Springbok prop and fellow great Os du Randt rated Hayman as the world's best tighthead, saying, "Playing against Carl, the next day you definitely knew about it."

Seismic gym sessions encompassing ludicrous weights created a mystique of their own and on-field success followed. Despite a toe infection that ruled him out of two Tests, Hayman beat the Lions twice in 2005 – once for New Zealand Maori and then again under Henry in Christchurch.

The following year he was a mainstay of a Tri-Nations triumph but a shock quarter-

final defeat to France derailed the 2007 World Cup mission. At the age of 27, Hayman had represented the All Blacks for the final time.

Although the NZRU tried a host of measures to keep him – CEO Steve Tew was forced to deny he had offered Hayman a dairy farm in Taranaki – he left for three lucrative seasons in England with Newcastle before joining Mourad Boudjellal at Toulon in 2010.

Signing off with three consecutive European titles, he fully vindicated rival tighthead Greg Somerville's assertion that "if he'd have stayed, he'd have played a helluva lot more Tests".

GRAHAM PRICE

MAJOR TEAMS: Pontypool

As a teenager, Graham Price was taken to the smoky bars of Pontypool and shown some of the pot-bellied beer drinkers who, once promising rugby players, had failed to make the most of their talent.

It was a message Price took to heart, and the youngster's appetite for hard work on the paddock was one element that helped propel him to stardom for club and country.

"Pricey worked like a dog in training and ran like a stag in games," said Terry Cobner, who captained Pontypool for a decade. "He had this huge resolve, an incredible single-mindedness and sense of purpose."

A Welsh Schools champion at shot and discus, Price made his first-team bow at Pontypool at 18 and started to learn the front-row ropes against grizzled and older opponents, many of them three stone heavier and not remotely inclined to go easy on a pup.

Price absorbed the lessons and became one of the greatest props the game has seen. He placed huge emphasis on the engagement, aiming to hit the top of the loosehead's head with his right shoulder and lock him in such an uncomfortable position that he was like putty in his hands.

Price liked to scrum just inches off the ground and the bigger the opponent, the more he relished folding them up like a used cereal packet. In a match on the 1980 Lions tour, the South Africans pitched the 6ft 4in, 23st heavyweight Flippie van der Merwe against him – and the Welshman had him on toast. "I remember one scrum in the second half where he let out a long wheeze that sounded like a death-rattle," Price recalls in *The Good, the Bad and the Ugly*.

Price played in two Grand Slam teams as well as 12 successive Lions Tests on the 1977, 1980 and 1983 tours. If little footage exists of his world-class scrummaging and mauling skills, at least there is one memorable clip: the try he scored on his Wales debut in Paris in 1975, when his hack and 70m chase culminated in him plunging over the line.

Position	Tighthead prop
Country	Wales
Test span	1975-83
Wales caps	41 (41 starts)
Lions caps	12 (12 starts)
Test points	12 (3T)

Price of success The Pontypool legend is the most-capped Lions front-row ever, with 12 Tests over three tours

TADHG FURLONG

Emerald star Furlong carries in last year's win v New Zealand

Position	Tighthead prop
Country	Ireland
Test span	2015-
Ireland caps	78
Lions caps	6
Test points	25 (5T)

MAJOR TEAMS: Leinster

It wasn't until he played for Ireland at an U20 World Cup that Tadhg Furlong realised he could mix it in exalted company. Until then, this farmer's son from Wexford was oblivious to how far his natural ball-playing talent could take him in professional sport.

Not that he was shy. Ireland U20 coach Mike Ruddock nicknamed him 'The Mayor of Wexford' but after Furlong won the team's Tackle of the Day for a third successive match, the prop asked to be dubbed 'The Jukebox' instead. When Ruddock asked why, Furlong replied, "Because the hits keep coming!"

He was right too because Furlong has carved his place among the best tightheads ever seen. At 6ft and 122kg, he has the perfect build for the modern No 3 and has forged a reputation as a square and patient scrummager able to win regular penalties in the set-piece.

His breakdown work is exemplary – just ask David Pocock, who he famously took out with a thunderous cleanout just as he was poised to make a vital turnover during the 2018 Australia-Ireland series.

Yet what separates Furlong from so many of his contemporaries is what he does with ball in hand, so much so that Ireland use him as a ball-carrier when prop forwards are usually deployed as support players.

Furlong has amazing agility for a big man and an acute awareness of space that owes something to his Gaelic football days. If a subtle offload is called for, he will deliver.

The player missed much of 2020 with calf and hamstring injuries yet made an immediate impact on his return. Against Scotland in last year's Six Nations, he stepped past both George Turner and Finn Russell with delightful sleight of foot, a manoeuvre that went viral on social media.

He was one of the first names on the team sheet for that summer's Lions series in South Africa, starting all three Tests. It had been the same story four years earlier, Furlong playing all but two minutes of the 2017 series against New Zealand and outwitting his opponent Joe Moody throughout.

Furlong was there for all three of Ireland's history-making defeats of the All Blacks, as well as the 2018 and 2023 Grand Slams. Where he goes, success will follow.

ROBERT PAPAREMBORDE

Pap star in Paris The Pau prop was Fran Cotton's nemesis – and the scourge of many

MAJOR TEAMS: Pau, Racing

Rated alongside Graham Price as "undoubtedly the greatest tighthead prop of the modern era" by another legend of the front row, Fran Cotton, Robert Paparemborde anchored a French pack that won three Five Nations titles, including Grand Slams in 1977 and 1981.

Known as the 'Bear of the Pyrenees', or Patou (which translates as a big, friendly dog), he didn't make his Test debut until he was 27 but was France's most-capped prop on his retirement and set a record for scoring tries from that position too.

Respected French coach Daniel Herrero credits Paparemborde with inventing modern prop play. He was mobile but more famously used his terrific strength to devastating effect in the scrum. "He was massively strong and powerful and had those incredible sloping shoulders that made him so difficult to scrummage against," recalls Cotton.

A judo black belt, he was a popular character who fellow prop Gérard Cholley credits as being the focal point of the France team in that era. He led les Bleus five times. Another comrade from that pack, Jean-Pierre Bastiat, said, "He was the most accomplished prop I ever saw."

France centre Roland Bertranne remembers Paparemborde asking the whole team to help choose a name for his daughter who was born on the day of a Test match, and they named her France.

Having spent most of his career with Pau, he switched to Racing in Paris for the final year, then coached them to the French title in 1990. He was also vice-president of the French federation, while away from rugby he was a shopkeeper, a bar owner and a local councillor in Pau.

Sadly, Paparemborde died from cancer at the age of just 52 in 2001, leaving behind his wife Valerie, son Pierre and daughters France and Elsa. He left a permanent and immense legacy for French rugby.

Position	Tighthead prop
Country	France
Test span	1975-83
Test caps	55 (55 starts)
Test points	32 (8T)

RUGBY LEGENDS

SECOND-ROWS

Not for nothing are the two 'locks' known as the engine room – it is they who provide the power in the scrum. The No 4 is typically shorter and bulkier, and often pushes behind the tighthead; you will jump at the front of the lineout and must be dynamic to react to a fast throw. In contrast, the No 5 will be a middle-of-the-lineout skyscraper able to win a stream of ball – and the same is required at restarts. Far from just being a big lump, a second row should be a clever clogs able to read the opposition or deceive them. And vertigo sufferers need not apply because you can be 13 feet off the ground when gathering in those lineout throws!

EBEN ETZEBETH

MAJOR TEAMS: Western Province, Stormers, Red Hurricanes Osaka, Toulon, Sharks

A towering, intimidating physical presence who combines power with world-class technique, the story of Etzebeth's career in the Springbok engine room is a record-breaking and unfinished one. He is already the most capped South African player ever and with two World Cup winner's medals, could yet become the first player in the game's history to become a triple world champion in 2027.

The young second row's eye-catching early performances for the Stormers earned him his Test debut against England in 2012 and despite his inexperience was nominated for the prestigious World Rugby Player of the Year award in 2013 before going on to make his World Cup bow two years later.

In Japan in 2019 Etzebeth scaled the pinnacle of the global game as the Springboks again faced the Red Rose in the World Cup final in Yokohama, the lock starting in his side's 32-12 triumph. In July 2022 he joined the 100-cap club when he faced Wales in Cape Town. In 2023 the second row joined a select group of players to win two World Cups as South Africa held their nerve in a tight, tense 12-11 victory over the All Blacks in the final in Paris.

The significant career milestones did not end there. In late 2024, Etzebeth made his 128th appearance for his country against Argentina, overtaking his former second-row team-mate Victor Matfield as the most capped Springbok ever. A peerless operator in the lineout and aggressive tackler, he played in every minute of all three Tests against the Lions in 2021.

He has twice won the Rugby Championship. His first winner's medal came in 2019 as the Springboks edged out the Wallabies for the title in a tournament truncated by the upcoming World Cup, and Etzebeth doubled up in 2024 when South Africa reigned supreme against their southern hemisphere rivals.

Position	Second-row
Country	South Africa
Test span	2012–
Test caps	131
Test points	35 (7T)

VICTOR MATFIELD

Brain and brawn Matfield tests the Pumas at RWC 2015

MAJOR TEAMS: Blue Bulls, Griquas, Cats, Toulon, Northampton Saints

Not even retirement halted Victor Matfield's influence on the Test stage. Two-and-a-half years after bowing out of rugby when the Springboks were dumped out of RWC 2011 by Australia, the shaggy-haired lock ended his hiatus and returned to Super Rugby action with the Blue Bulls, for whom he had been serving as a lineout coach.

That June, Matfield captained South Africa to a defeat of a World XV in Cape Town at the age of 37 and promptly added to his impressive tally of 110 caps in the ensuing two-Test series against Wales.

Four months later, he played all 80 minutes of an epic 27-25 victory over New Zealand at Ellis Park. It was the All Blacks' first loss in 22 outings and provided indisputable evidence that Matfield could still mix it with the best on the planet.

Position	Second-row
Country	South Africa
Test span	2001-15
Test caps	127 (121 starts)
Test points	35 (7T)

In truth, his status as a lock legend was secure long before he finally hung up his boots four days shy of his 39th birthday at Northampton. Matfield's mathematical set-piece prowess in a complementary engine-room partnership with bruising Bakkies Botha was a mainstay of the 2007 World Cup success and 2009 series defeat of the Lions.

In between, he led the Springboks to a defeat of New Zealand in 2008, ending their five-year unbeaten home record. There were also three Super Rugby titles in four years with the Bulls in a period drenched with silverware on all fronts.

The most-capped Springbok ever, Matfield named Paul O'Connell as his most respected opponent. The Irishman wasted no time in returning the compliment: "He's the best lineout forward in the world and has been for a long time. To be able to take two years out and come back as good, if not better, than ever is an incredible achievement."

MARTIN JOHNSON

Ultimate prize Johnson accepts the Webb Ellis Cup in 2003

MAJOR TEAMS: Leicester, King Country

With his furrowed brow, imposing 6ft 7in, 18st 9lb frame and a stare that could curdle cream from a hundred yards, Martin Johnson was England's enforcer and most successful captain. When he lifted the World Cup in 2003, it was his 39th Test as captain – of which England had won 34.

His leadership credentials had been apparent since 1997 when Ian McGeechan picked the Leicester lock to lead the Lions into what ended as a triumphant series.

Johnson had made his name four years earlier on the Lions tour of New Zealand – after just one cap for England. The land of the long white cloud had already had a profound effect on Johnson. As a teenager he had been approached by Colin Meads to try out for King Country and spent two years there honing his craft.

Solihull-born, Johnson resumed a 16-year love affair with Welford Road, playing 362 games for the Tigers and leading them to two Heineken Cups and four Premiership titles.

His ability to read a game whilst it unfolded, communicating to team-mates the course of action most likely to bring a try a few phases down the line, was remarkable. "His rugby brain was a huge component in making him a great captain," said former Tiger Geordan Murphy.

In 2001 Johnson became the first player to lead a Lions squad twice, and two years later, after a second England Grand Slam, he was part of a rearguard action that beat the Kiwis on their own soil for the first time since 1973. John Eales called his performance "among the best ever by a lock forward".

After driving England to their defining moment in Sydney, Johnson retired at the end of that season. Despite his lack of coaching experience, he became England manager and steered them to a Six Nations title in 2011, before stepping down following that year's World Cup in New Zealand.

Position	Second-row
Country	England
Test span	1993-2003
England caps	84 (82 starts)
Lions caps	8 (8 starts)
Test points	10 (2T)

FRIK DU PREEZ

MAJOR TEAMS: Northern Transvaal

When Frik du Preez and All Black Colin Meads locked the scrum for a President's Overseas XV against England in 1971 in a match to celebrate the centenary of the RFU, many thought they would never see a better pairing in tandem.

The crowd certainly thought so and gave the pair a standing ovation when they left the pitch. It was a rare treat for the fans and in the modern day could arguably only be equalled if John Eales and Martin Johnson were on the same side.

Du Preez was voted South African Rugby Player of the 20th century by Springbok fans. His Test career ran from 1961 to 1971, and South Africa won a World Cup in 1995, so for him to be held in such esteem decades after he had played his last Test proves what affection the South African public have for the man.

Du Preez was a brute of a lock who put the fear of God into the opposition. He performed all the duties expected of him but could kick goals and run with the ball as well, as the Lions found out in the first Test of 1968 when du Preez sprinted in for a try from nearly 50 metres.

The man from Northern Transvaal had announced himself to the public while serving as an officer in the South African Air Force and played for the Defence Force side against Pretoria. The legendary Salty du Rand was in the opposition and the young upstart gave him a chasing that launched a Boks career encompassing 87 games, including 38 Tests.

By the time he signed off in Sydney, he was the most-capped Springbok and the Sydney Morning Herald wrote that du Preez was "what Bradman was to Australian cricket, Pele was to Latin American football and Colin Meads is to New Zealand rugby".

Position	Second-row
Country	South Africa
Test span	1961-71
Test caps	38 (38 starts)
Test points	11 (1T, 1C, 2P)

Frik of nature Du Preez was one of only two Boks voted into the Rugby Hall of Fame when it was created in 1997

MAJOR TEAMS: West of Scotland

Few personalities come as big as Gordon Brown – or 'Broon frae Troon', as he will forever be remembered.

The son of a Scottish goalkeeping father and international hockey-playing mother, the 6ft 5in Brown was a mighty set-piece forward with surprising skills with ball in hand. His brother Peter also packed down for Scotland in the second row, and Gordon became the first Scot to replace his brother as a sub, against Wales in 1970.

GORDON BROWN

Buffalo charge Brown runs at Ray Gravell during the Scots' 1975 win v Wales

Large and hardy, he often ended up in the mix when things got tough. However, it was Brown's warmth and gregariousness off the field that saw him elevated to the pantheon of British greats. After all, this was Willie John McBride's right-hand man for the victorious Lions tour of South Africa in 1974, and he also helped the side to that historic series win over New Zealand in 1971.

It was on the '74 tour that one of the most famous stories about Brown originated. In one dicey match, Brown hit Johan de Bruyn, a big man with a glass eye. It shot out and as a result both teams and the match official halted play to try to find the eye on the turf. When de Bruyn eventually found it and popped it back in, Brown delighted in telling audiences for years afterwards, a tuft of grass was also sticking out of the socket.

Brown scored nine tries on that tour – including two in the Test series – and five years later his career ended with another tour of New Zealand. By that point his Scotland stint was fizzling out.

Position	Second-row
Country	Scotland
Test span	1969-77
Scotland caps	30 (28 starts)
Lions caps	8 (8 starts)
Test points	8 (2T)

In 2001 he succumbed to cancer at the age of 53. His passing shocked the sport – this was a player who Welsh hardman Bobby Windsor said "I love you" to and to whom de Bruyn later presented the famous glass eye as a gift – but he was remembered with fondness. "He was a big man in every sense," said Scotland legend Jim Telfer.

Brown was a raconteur who liked the post-match festivities, but he was also the rugby players' rugby player – a battler – and Scotland's greatest-ever lock.

PAUL O'CONNELL

MAJOR TEAMS: Munster

Superman heads to bed each night wearing Paul O'Connell pyjamas, or so the story goes down in Limerick. Certainly, Clark Kent's alter ego might be frightened to don anything else.

According to Ronan O'Gara, O'Connell's long-term lieutenant with Munster and Ireland, it is a relentless dedication that characterises the lock. "Paul is all about standards," says the former fly-half. "I've seen what difference one individual can make to an organisation."

O'Connell exudes an intelligent but fiercely authoritative charisma. Inspirational leadership underpins a staggering honours list – two Heineken Cups, a century of Ireland caps, three Lions tours and another trio of Six Nations titles that includes the 2009 Grand Slam.

Standing 6ft 6in tall, physical presence contributes something primal to his aura. One changing room address to his Ireland team-mates prior to a clash with France has had over a million views on YouTube. In it, he urged "manic aggression", asking colleagues to ask themselves the question: "Did I put the fear of God into anyone?"

Returning from a debilitating back injury to give a Man of the Match display for Munster against Harlequins in a 2013 Heineken Cup quarter-final, O'Connell showed himself ready for a third Lions tour to Australia after heading to New Zealand in 2005 and captaining the 2009 South Africa trip. In the wake of that monstrous effort, he said, "I felt like an amateur today" – a declaration of the burning pride he felt in representing his province.

Defeat by Glasgow in the 2015 Pro12 final ended O'Connell's Munster career with a solitary Celtic League title, and there was more heartache that year at the World Cup when he suffered a horrific hamstring injury against France. It not only ended his 13-year Test career but prevented him taking up a two-year contract with Toulon.

"He's simply irreplaceable," said Brian O'Driscoll when O'Connell announced his retirement and embarked on a coaching career that now sees him in charge of Ireland's forwards.

Position	Second-row
Country	Ireland
Test span	2002-15
Ireland caps	108 (99 starts)
Lions caps	7 (7 starts)
Test points	40 (8T)

Halting a hulk Two Wallabies battle to bring O'Connell down

COLIN MEADS

Enforcer Meads played rugby with brutal intensity

MAJOR TEAMS: King Country

Sir Colin Meads, through his rugby achievements, was probably the greatest All Black of them all.

He set a world record by appearing in 55 Internationals, including New Zealand's 17-Test winning streak from 1965-69, and in all played 133 times for the All Blacks, a national record that stood for more than 40 years.

For his hardness and implacability he was known as 'Pinetree'. Meads put his strength down to the outdoor demands of his hillside stock farm in King Country. His arms were longer than average, giving him an advantage levering the ball free from mauls. And on the hoof, flourishing the ball in one hand, he was a fearsome sight for opponents.

Today's TV scrutiny would have forced him to rein in the darker side of his game. At Murrayfield in 1967 he became only the second man to be sent off in a major Test, and his enthusiasm for removing bodies on the wrong side of rucks outraged Aussies when he dragged their captain, Ken Catchpole, with such brute force that the Wallaby had to retire from rugby.

But Meads could also take the rough stuff. When his head was lacerated by a French boot in 1967 he played on, and when his arm was broken by a kick in South Africa in 1970 he again played on. No player had such a high pain threshold.

Barry John once put Meads's standing in context. "A hundred years from now," the Welsh legend wrote, "when men are discussing the all-time greats, Colin Meads will be near the top of the list."

Position	Second-row
Country	New Zealand
Test span	1957-71
Test caps	55 (55 starts)
Test points	21 (7T)

WILLIE JOHN MCBRIDE

MAJOR TEAMS: Ballymena, Ulster

Not the least of Willie John McBride's battery of achievements is that he didn't even play rugby until 17 – yet within five years was a fully fledged Ireland and Lions international. That fact tells you much about the Ulsterman who was to play more Lions Tests (17) and make more Lions appearances (70) than any other man, as well as make a joint-record five Lions tours.

McBride's childhood laid the foundation of his stellar career, for on the family farm he acquired a work ethic and sense of unity that transferred to his rugby. Losing his dad at four, McBride and his older brothers worked tirelessly; he once cut and stacked corn through the night prior to undertaking his daily three-mile walk to school.

Initially McBride was a beanpole No 8 but he filled out to become a fearsome lock with no respect for reputations. On his third cap, in France, he played with a broken leg for 30 minutes and, at 23, irritated by being pushed in a lineout by an All Black, he belted the culprit – Colin Meads.

McBride was a warrior, never willing to take a backward step. Having scored the only try of the 1968 Lions series in South Africa, he turned the tables on the southern hemisphere in 1971 in New Zealand (2-1).

Appointed Ireland captain in 1973, he led the 1974 Lions aged 34, and his stirring speeches and diplomatic skills came to the fore as the tourists won 3-0. His initiation of the '99' call, to quash opposition thuggery at source through all-in retaliation, has passed into legend.

Fellow Lion Andy Ripley said, "Why did we all love Willie so much? Because he unreservedly loved all 30 of us. He made us feel like we'd just won the pools." After clinching the series, McBride made the Test team go over to the dirt-trackers in the stand and applaud them.

A banker all his working life, McBride played for Ballymena across four decades and later coached Ulster and Ireland, as well as managing the 1983 Lions.

Position	Second-row
Country	Ireland
Test span	1962-75
Ireland caps	63 (63 starts)
Lions caps	17 (17 starts)
Test points	7 (2T)

Indomitable McBride is a Lions giant and in 2004 was named Rugby Personality of the Century by *Rugby World*

JOHN EALES

MAJOR TEAMS: Brothers, Queensland

His famous nickname, 'Nobody', as in 'nobody's perfect', is a myth, because none of his mates call him that. But everything else you hear about the wonder that is John Eales is true, which explains why many regard him as Australia's greatest-ever rugby player.

The Queenslander showed remarkable lineout athleticism at a young age, with England second-row Paul Ackford highlighting the youngster's ability to make space for himself in such a claustrophobic area shortly before the first of Eales's 86 caps in July 1991.

Eales was just 20 when he made his Test debut and, though his scrum power and general mobility took a little while to develop, within months he was playing in a World Cup. Coach Bob Dwyer, who had quickly abandoned an experiment to turn him into a No 8, was vindicated by a series of outstanding performances. Together with Rod McCall, Eales won the lineouts 28-2 against Wales, and his try-saving tackle on England's Rob Andrew in the final drew gasps from the crowd – 6ft 7in locks weren't meant to do that!

His kicking had already come to notice thanks to an amazing 45m drop-goal for his club Brothers, and a couple of blinding slip catches in a cricket match convinced Queensland coach John Connolly that Eales had the coordination to be a goalkicker – he was to kick 164 Test points, including the late penalty that won the 2000 Bledisloe Cup.

Named Wallaby captain at the start of the Greg Smith era in 1996, Eales was to lead his country 55 times – putting him tenth on the all-time list. His high point was a second world title back on British soil in 1999, when he became one of only six men at that point to achieve a World Cup double.

He had time to beat the Lions before retiring as the most capped second-row in history, a record since surpassed. Wallaby team-mate Jason Little once said, "It got to the point where I thought Ealsey was going to kick off, catch it himself, go all the way, score the try and kick the goal!" He was echoing the thoughts of many.

Taking the silver Eales hoists the 2001 Bledisloe Cup

Position	Second-row
Country	Australia
Test span	1991-2001
Test caps	86 (86 starts)
Test points	173 (2T, 31C, 34P)

ALUN WYN JONES

Heart of the action Alun Wyn Jones looks to offload against the Stormers on last year's Lions tour

MAJOR TEAMS: Ospreys

It sounds strange to say that stats fail to convey Alun Wyn Jones's value to the sport because those stats are remarkable. Nobody else has played 161 Tests, 12 of them coming in four successive Lions series and placing him behind only Willie John McBride and Dickie Jeeps in that esteemed appearances list.

The Osprey has also played in four World Cups and been present for all four Welsh Grand Slams this century – he watched the first one in 2005 from behind the goalposts.

None of which explains why team-mates and opponents alike are unanimous in admiration for the 36-year-old Welshman. "He's an awesome man," says All Blacks captain Sam Whitelock. "What he's done for his club and country, and the way he puts it on the line every week, is amazing."

The second-row position doesn't lend itself to flash moments, and that suits AWJ just fine. His on-field excellence is illustrated via chasing kicks and hitting rucks, making tackles and winning restarts – energy and effort that rubs off on all around him.

It's not just on match day that he drives the standards. Toby Booth relates how when he arrived as Ospreys coach, he thought AWJ was trying to impress him given the bewildering markers he was setting in training. The back-room staff knew otherwise. "They went 'That's Al'," Booth says. "Every time, every minute – I wish there were more like him."

Position	Second-row
Country	Wales
Test span	2006-2023
Wales caps	158 (142 starts)
Lions caps	12 (10 starts)
Test points	45 (9T)

There's only one Alun Wyn of course, and it's doubtful that any other player would have recovered from the dislocated shoulder he incurred against Japan last year to rejoin the Lions tour as captain. The most optimistic prognosis was a three-month absence post surgery. Instead, he decided to rehab the injury himself and installed altitude equipment and a hyperbaric chamber at his house. Daily physio, then collision work ten days on from the scans, led to him playing for the Lions just 21 days after the Japan mishap. It was a rugby miracle more in keeping with Lourdes. Following the Six Nations in 2023, Wyn Jones announced his retirement, drawing to a close his historic and record-breaking career.

RUGBY LEGENDS

BLINDSIDE FLANKERS

Did you enjoy mucking about in flowerbeds as a toddler, emerging from the garden covered in mud? Welcome to the world of blindside flankers, the players who do the dirty work. The No 6's raison d'être is to tackle, tackle, tackle – you are there to destroy so that colleagues can create. Bigger and slower than the openside, you will be happiest mixing it with the heavy guys close to the rucks, mauls and set-piece; big hits and ruck clean-outs are your staple. Coaches sometimes tinker with the back-row balance but whoever they select, the unit must always contain somebody who picks up that shovel and does the hard graft.

ALAN WHETTON

MAJOR TEAMS: Auckland

Alan Whetton was a mainstay of the All Blacks in the Eighties, playing many of his 35 Tests alongside twin brother Gary, who plied his trade in the engine room.

Whetton's early appearances wearing the Silver Fern were inauspicious as he came on as a replacement in his first four Tests, then incurred a two-match ban for playing on a 'rebel' Cavaliers tour to South Africa.

Worse was to come on his full debut in 1986 against Australia. Disappointed by his performance, he overdid the post-match port and in a state of insobriety had to be escorted to bed before the official dinner.

Position	Blindside flanker
Country	New Zealand
Test span	1984-91
Test caps	35 (31 starts)
Test points	40 (10T)

Breaking away Whetton steps the Wallabies No.11, All Blacks v Australia, Concord Oval, 3 July 1988

Rather than mope and lament his poor judgment, it was the making of him, as he got fit and forced his way into the line-up for Brian Lochore's 1987 World Cup squad.

Playing in a feted back row alongside Buck Shelford and Michael Jones, the triumvirate proved a formidable unit as New Zealand swatted aside the likes of Italy, Wales and Scotland. Whetton had a notable tournament, scoring in every game except the final against France at his home ground with Auckland, Eden Park. That was ironic as he had a pre-match ritual there designed to boost his scoring. "I'd go to each corner and imagine myself dotting down. I'd pat the grass and think, 'That could be AJ's spot'."

He was renowned for his support play, pace on the short side and work at the breakdown, and he remained a fixture in the team until bowing out in the RWC 1991 semi-final against the Wallabies.

Domestically, he played for Auckland more than 150 times before retiring to take up a three-year coaching stint with Kobe Steelers in Japan. He also played for West Hartlepool in England, along with Gary, and carved a path in digital sports signage at stadiums.

ROGER UTTLEY

MAJOR TEAMS: Fylde, Gosforth, Wasps

Roger Uttley was a granite-like forward who made his name on the Lions tour of South Africa in 1974 when he was taken as a lock but played all four Tests in the back row. He played all but one of the 17 tour games and scored a crucial try in the final, drawn Test.

The Blackpool-born Uttley had been in England's second row in 1973 and 1974, playing in the wins over New Zealand (in Auckland) and Australia – rare highlights in a poor period for English rugby.

A schoolteacher at Harrow, where he was director of physical education, Uttley didn't tour with the Lions in 1977 because of injury but soldiered on with England, captaining them five times. They won their first Grand Slam for 23 years in 1980 when, in the view of coach Mike Davis, Uttley was one of five world-class players in the team.

Position	Blindside flanker
Country	England
Test span	1973-80
England caps	23 (23 starts)
Lions caps	4 (4 starts)
Test points	12 (3T)

The defeat of Wales saw Uttley incur a terrible injury. Geoff Wheel tried to kick the ball but connected with the flanker's head instead, splitting his nose. "Tony Neary came over and said, 'Christ!'. My face felt like a football," recalls Uttley.

Regular injuries were part and parcel of Uttley's career, notably an ongoing back problem that first arose when he trod on some uneven turf during a training session in Scotland. He has a long back due to an extra sacrum vertebra.

The 30-18 defeat of Scotland in Edinburgh that clinched the Grand Slam signalled the end of his England career, but he was to enjoy some great times as a coach. He was an assistant to Ian McGeechan as the pair plotted the Lions' win over the Wallabies in 1989 and coached England to the 1991 World Cup final at Twickenham alongside Geoff Cooke.

In 1997 Uttley was appointed England team manager under their first full-time head coach, Clive Woodward, but he lost that job two years later following a swathe of cost-cutting measures by the RFU. A tireless charity fund-raiser (he's a member of the Wooden Spoon children's charity), he remained at Harrow until 2008. Now retired, he is an enthusiastic recreational cyclist.

Hard as nails Uttley never let an injury stop him

RICHARD HILL

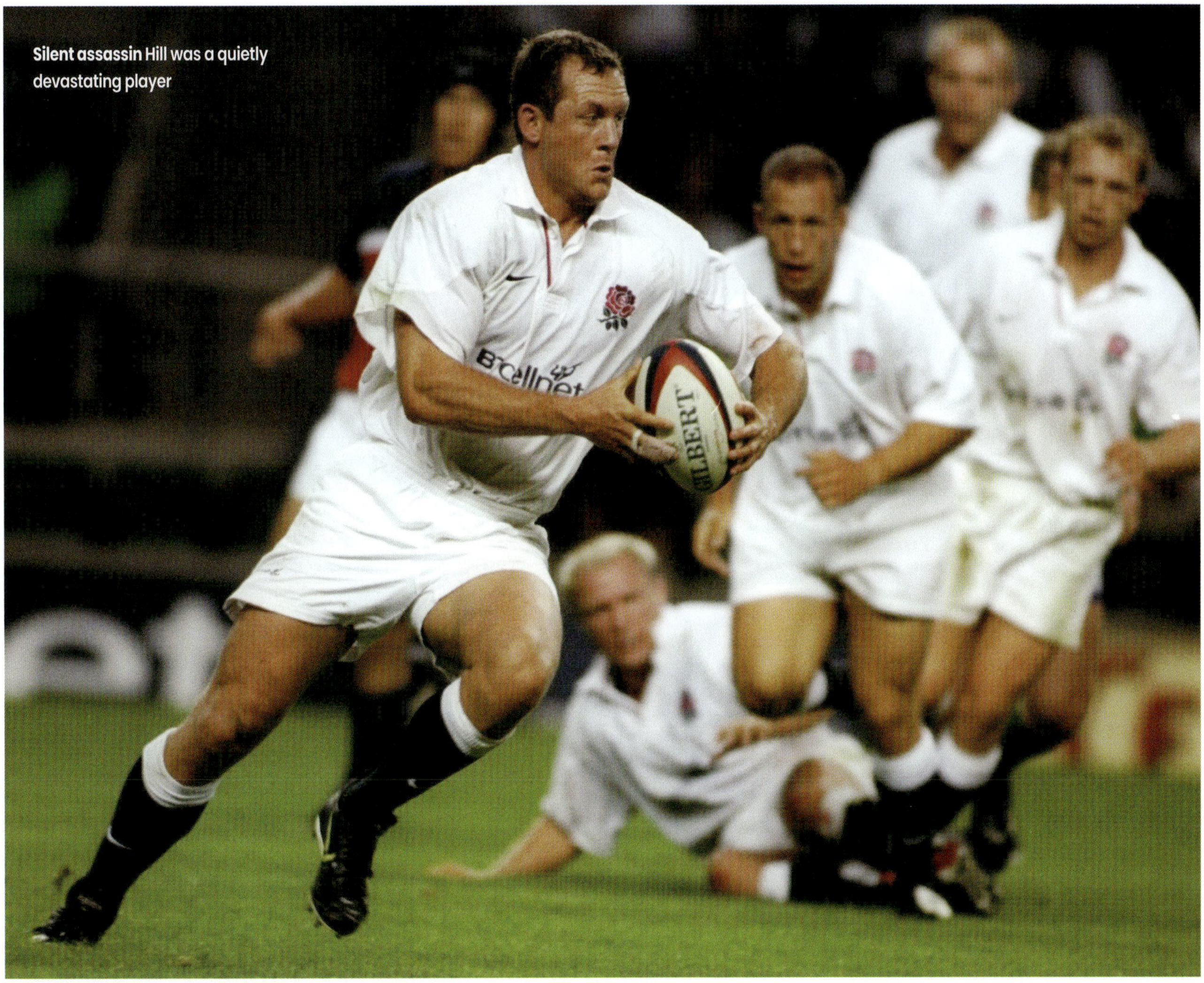

Silent assassin Hill was a quietly devastating player

MAJOR TEAMS: Saracens

Soon after joining Saracens in 1993, Richard Hill was asked by coach John Davies what he would do if Mike Teague, the Moseley back-row, came thundering towards him in the upcoming match? Davies was looking for a suitably aggressive reply but Hill merely answered: "Hopefully I'll get in a good position to tackle him."

Hill always was understated, but he got in good positions time and time again for England and the Lions. This selfless back-rower was called the unsung hero of the great England team of the early 2000s, yet the many tributes to him make a mockery of the tag.

Initially an openside, in which role he played for the victorious 1997 Lions in South Africa, Hill became one of the all-time great No 6s after Clive Woodward implemented the legendary Dallaglio-Hill-Back unit at half-time against New Zealand during his second Test in charge.

Hill's decision-making and technique at the breakdown provided the oil for England's engine. He had all the skills – he kicked goals as a youngster and scored 12 Test tries – but it was in the tight exchanges that he came into his own. He seldom lost his individual battles.

Woodward never dropped him and when Hill damaged a hamstring in the RWC 2003 opener against Georgia, the coach refused to summon a replacement. Hill had played only a game and a half since June when he played in the November semi-final, and two years later he was picked for the Lions after only two halves of rugby in six months – that's how important he was.

Once chased by Wigan RL after scoring a hat-trick in a divisional match, Hill hailed from the Salisbury club but played all his pro rugby for Saracens, making 288 appearances.

Sadly, injuries featured heavily in his career, such as the concussion halfway through the 2001 Lions series that many believe turned events Australia's way. An ACL injury sustained in 2004 would have finished most people, but remarkably Hill battled on after two knee reconstructions before finally accepting the inevitable. Today he is the England team manager.

Position	Blindside flanker
Country	England
Test span	1997-2005
England caps	71 (68 starts)
Lions caps	5 (5 starts)
Test points	60 (12T)

MIKE TEAGUE

Blood, sweat and tears Teague releases the ball during the RWC 1991 semi-final win against Scotland

MAJOR TEAMS: Gloucester, Moseley, Cardiff, Stroud

Dubbed 'Iron Mike' by former England second-row Paul Ackford, Mike Teague is a god in Gloucester, a hero for England and a legend for the Lions.

His finest hour was the 1989 Lions tour to Australia, when he missed the first-Test defeat through injury but came back to wear the No 6 jersey to such great effect in the next two Tests that he was voted Man of the Series as the tourists achieved a come-from-behind triumph for the first and only time.

Teague had only established himself in the England team that spring. He won his first three caps in 1985, aged 25, but was then left out until the 1989 Five Nations. He responded by bulking up and taking his fitness to new levels with what Gloucester folk call 'Mad Dog' training, involving hill running over all kinds of terrain carrying rocks and logs.

The gruelling work enabled him to play his trademark physical game on what was, at times, a violent Lions tour and Teague turned the tide in the visitors' favour. Socks rolled down, he tackled everything that moved, was a driving force in the loose and a limpet in possession. "He was sensational to watch. Blood, sweat and tears was Teaguey," said former team-mate Jeremy Guscott.

Position	Blindside flanker
Country	England
Test span	1985-93
England caps	27 (26 starts)
Lions caps	3 (2 starts)
Test points	15 (3T)

In 1991 he scored two tries on the way to a Grand Slam and a World Cup final, and two years later he played another Test for the Lions, finishing with a 100% win record for the tourists after beating New Zealand 20-7.

Teague joined Gloucester from the All Blues club as a teenager in 1978 and played 301 times for the first team over the next 17 years. He had short spells at Stroud and Cardiff, and two seasons with Moseley from 1992.

As a self-employed builder during his playing days, he now owns Teague Construction and maintains close ties with Gloucester RFC, once co-owning Teague's Bar, opposite Kingsholm.

SCHALK BURGER

Burger king The Springbok was a savage competitor

MAJOR TEAMS: Western Province, Stormers, Suntory Sungoliath, Saracens

Schalk Burger's presence in our Blindsides list may seem incongruous, given he started out as a No 8 and played at openside in his early, blistering years of Test rugby. But South Africa have traditionally adopted a 'left' and 'right' flanker, and in any case Burger excelled across the whole of the back row, becoming a link man in his twilight playing days with Premiership club Saracens.

"I've always tried to evolve, tried to add depth to my game," Burger told Rugby World shortly before he retired in 2019. "I've tried to be an all-rounder. When I play well, my stats will be spread out between carries, tackles, cleans and passes."

Appropriately, the blond bombshell exploded into the public consciousness. Graduating from the renowned rugby nurseries of Paarl Gimnasium and Stellenbosch University, Burger was part of the South Africa U21 side that won the 2002 World Championship.

The following year he broke into the Western Province team and played at the World Cup in Australia, scoring on his Test debut against Georgia.

When Jake White took over in 2004, he unleashed the gap-toothed, grinning youngster and ogled at the effects. So destructive was Burger against Ireland that losing coach Eddie O'Sullivan said he had seldom experienced a Test series when one player beat 15. That year South Africa won the Tri-Nations for the first time in six seasons. Hurtling into rucks and runners alike, Burger won World Player of the Year at the age of 21.

Burger would drive the Boks to World Cup glory in 2007, though this would be sandwiched between two serious setbacks – a neck injury that required cervical fusion surgery in 2006 and life-threatening bacterial meningitis in 2013.

Against Wales in 2014, Burger ended a two-and-a-half-year Test hiatus. Five months on, he burrowed over to help beat England 31-28 at Twickenham. He became the 55th Springbok captain in 2015, playing in his fourth World Cup. Only three men – Jason Leonard, Richie McCaw and Alun Wyn Jones – have chalked up more World Cup appearances. New Zealand legend Sean Fitzpatrick attributed Burger's remarkable recovery to his immense "fighting spirit". Either side of the touchline, undiluted tenacity served him very well indeed.

Position	Blindside flanker
Country	South Africa
Test span	2003-15
Test caps	86 (72 starts)
Test points	80 (16T)

JERRY COLLINS

MAJOR TEAMS: Wellington, Hurricanes, Ospreys, Toulon, Yamaha, Narbonne

There are back-rows who have been capped more, players with World Cups to their names and players who perhaps have toed the line more, but few had the impact or indeed cult following of Jerry Collins.

Born in Samoa, Collins moved to Auckland as a child. Rugby ran in his blood, with All Black Tana Umaga a cousin, so it was no surprise that he breezed through the New Zealand age grades.

On the field he was ferocious and utterly relentless, with his distinctive bleached blond 'Guinness' top acting as a warning beacon for attackers. But off the pitch he was a warm, unconventional figure happier sharing a pint with a few locals than playing up to the celebrity lifestyle.

Collins played his Super Rugby with the Hurricanes but was best known to northern hemisphere fans as part of a daunting All

Black back-row unit with Richie McCaw and Rodney So'oialo.

"He's one of the most special players who will ever wear a black jersey," said All Black great Michael Jones. "He took the No 6 jersey to new dimensions. The game became a lot more physical and confrontational. Jerry brought that level of physicality and brutal influence."

Collins played in two World Cups and won five Tri-Nations tournaments, where his uncompromising style won him many admirers. Despite his happy-go-lucky persona, he captained the All Blacks three times before retiring from Test duty in 2007 to seek adventure in Europe.

In 2008 he turned out for Barnstaple after a chance conversation in a pub, and after a year with Toulon he headed to Wales with the Ospreys, driving them to the Pro12 title. There followed a stint in Japan with Yamaha Engines Jubilo until, at 32, he left rugby to work in security in Canada.

He was drawn back to rugby for a final hurrah after an offer from French D2 side Narbonne. Tragically, in 2015 he was killed in a car crash in the South of France with his wife Alana, sparking widespread grief. He was taken far too soon.

Position	Blindside flanker
Country	New Zealand
Test span	2001-07
Test caps	48 (42 starts)
Test points	25 (5T)

SIMON POIDEVIN

MAJOR TEAMS: Randwick, Waratahs

Simon Poidevin isn't the first name to spring to mind when recalling the Wallaby side of the early Nineties, but the 'boy from the bush' was the back-row glue that all great teams covet.

The flanker from the NSW country town of Goulburn was almost freakishly fit, his ability to get on the inside shoulders of Mark Ella and Michael Lynagh on the 1984 Wallabies tour bringing him a try at Twickenham – one of six during his Test career.

A strong ball-carrier who could occupy three defenders, Poidevin boasted a prodigious tackle rate and an obsessive refusal to accept defeat. Ella rated him Australia's best player for years – "He's such a perfectionist, it's almost a disease," he said – while Grand Slam-winning coach Alan Jones went even further: "For his commitment, competitiveness, discipline, will to win and determination to perfect skills, he is without peer in modern rugby."

Sport is in Poidevin's blood. A descendent of a French wine merchant, his grandfather was selected for the first Wallaby tour to Britain in 1908, while a great uncle was the first Australian batsman to score 100 centuries at all levels of cricket.

Comfortable on both flanks, the Randwick player stood toe to toe with the formidable All Blacks side of the mid-1980s, helping the Wallabies win the Bledisloe Cup on foreign soil in 1986. He captained his country in the same year but was bitterly disappointed at Australia's fourth-place finish at the following year's inaugural World Cup and chose to retire from the Test stage.

Coach Bob Dwyer was never going to accept that. By 1991 Poidevin was installed in Dwyer's World Cup XV, and his tireless scavenging and unbreakable spirit in the face of a bigger English pack in the final were crucial to Australia's triumph. Even after getting wiped out by Mickey Skinner, Poidevin just smiled and came back for more.

It was to be the final Test outing for the player given the sobriquet 'The King'.

Position	Blindside flanker
Country	Australia
Test span	1980-91
Test caps	59 (59 starts)
Test points	24 (6T)

Perfectionist Poidevin at the 1987 World Cup. Wallaby coach Alan Jones rated him "without peer" in the Eighties

MAJOR TEAMS: Lourdes

France suffered an inferiority complex as international rugby's 'also-rans' for nearly 50 years before Jean Prat became their skipper in 1953. The olive-skinned, Lourdes-born flanker was the leader they had been crying out for and Five Nations glory soon materialised.

Prat's credentials for captaincy were impeccable. He had already inspired the miracle city to two French club titles before picking up the national reins, while as a seasoned Test player of

JEAN PRAT

Monsieur Rugby Prat led France to their first Five Nations title successes

courage, determination and stamina – legacies of his rural upbringing and love of cross-country running – he led by example.

Early in his tenure France recorded their maiden success against the All Blacks, Prat himself scoring the only try of a Paris win in 1954, and three Five Nations victories that season conferred (shared) Championship honours on France for the first time.

There was another shared title in 1955 when Prat took France to the brink of a Grand Slam, Wales depriving them of the holy grail at the end of the season.

Another player who could equally have made our Opensides list, Prat instigated a tight-marking policy with an attacking base off the back row. His exhortations to do this, that and everything sometimes left colleagues bewildered. At Twickenham, prop Amédée Domenech felt so overwhelmed that, finding himself unexpectedly in possession, he threw the ball at his captain with a hopeful remark: "Here, what can you do with it?" Prat promptly dropped a goal to seal a 16-9 victory!

All told, Prat won 51 caps between 1945 and 1955, scoring 144 points (a then-record for a forward) and was remarkably adept at dropping goals – including two in that triumph at Twickenham in 1955.

After retirement, he coached Lourdes to further successes, served as France's technical adviser for a famous 8-6 Test win in South Africa in 1964 and was so revered by his countrymen that they called him "Monsieur Rugby". No Frenchman was ever more deserving of the title.

Position	Blindside flanker
Country	France
Test span	1945-55
Test caps	51 (51 starts)
Test points	144 (9T, 27C, 15P, 6DG)

JOHN JEFFREY

MAJOR TEAMS: Kelso

Ceaselessly circling the breakdown, ruthlessly attacking on the counter or nibbling at opponents when he felt they needed winding up, there is more to John Jeffrey's nickname of 'White Shark' than just his shock-blond hair and pale skin.

A hero of the Borders – where it's hard to envisage the Kelso farmer ever having to put his hand in his pocket at the local pub – Jeffrey played more often like an auxiliary openside, relishing Scotland's high-tempo, ruck-driven style of the 1980s and early 1990s. He was relentless, popping up when you least expected him like the Jaws of the silver screen.

Jeffrey had a knack for try-scoring and when he retired was not only Scotland's most-capped flanker but shared the record with Derek White for most tries with 11. His haul included four at RWC 1987 and two against Samoa in 1991.

Yet he is best known for his high jinks with England No 8 Dean Richards, as the pair, fresh from the 1988 Calcutta Cup match, damaged the old trophy during a night on the tiles in Edinburgh. Jeffrey copped a five-month ban. But Jeffrey always bit back. He toured with the 1989 Lions and bagged two tries against Australia A, but he couldn't force his way into the team as the coaches adopted an English-type mauling game over the rucking style that was favoured by the Scots.

The next year he was to the fore as Scotland sealed a Grand Slam after their immortal 13-7 victory over England at Murrayfield. Seeing Jeffrey that day, snarling, sprinting and battering, was to see him at his best. Jeffrey is chairman of the Scottish Rugby Board and the Six Nations Council.

Position	Blindside flanker
Country	Scotland
Test span	1984-91
Test caps	40 (40 starts)
Test points	44 (11T)

Shark attack Jeffrey carries against France for Scotland in 1990

IAN KIRKPATRICK

Hallowed name Kirkpatrick was inducted into World Rugby's Hall of Fame in 2014

MAJOR TEAMS: Poverty Bay, Canterbury

Sometimes a player leaves an indelible imprint on the game, making a change that outlasts his own playing days. All Black Ian Kirkpatrick belongs to that select band.

When he emerged in the mid-Sixties, flankers usually played left and right, rather than openside and blindside, but Kirkpatrick helped shape the role of the blindside flanker as we know it today.

A farmer, he learned his rugby at Auckland's Kings College, joined the Poverty Bay club at 20 in 1966, then moved to Canterbury a year later. Coach Fred Allen capped him on tour in France that year, Kirkpatrick notching a try on debut as New Zealand prevailed 21-15 in Colombes.

A year later he became the first All Black to be used as a substitute, coming on when Brian Lochore broke his thumb in Sydney. Having warmed up by running down the stairs from the reserve seats, Kirkpatrick shredded the Wallaby defence to score a hat-trick in a 27-11 win. For the next nine years he was one of the first names on the All Blacks team sheet.

Tall and athletic, his uninhibited, dynamic style brought him 115 tries in 289 first-class games, including 16 in Tests – an All Blacks record until Stuart Wilson bettered it in 1983. His most spectacular score was the 55m burst out of a maul against the 1971 Lions in the Christchurch second Test.

Position	Blindside flanker
Country	New Zealand
Test span	1967-77
Test caps	39 (38 starts)
Test points	57 (16T)

Kirkpatrick later reflected on his superb try: "Pinetree (Colin Meads) always said he had a part to play in that because he gave me the ball. They came at me and I was able to push them off until I hit the corner."

He needed an injection to play in the next Test having injured a rib whilst handling a farm horse. He led New Zealand in nine Tests in 1972-73 prior to finishing in triumph against the 1977 Lions.

Kirkpatrick retired in 1979 but has stayed involved with rugby via media work, as a mentor for young players and as a patron of the Ngatapa club. He was inducted into the Hall of Fame and more recently was named New Zealand Rugby's patron after the death of Sir Brian Lochore in 2019.

SIYA KOLISI

MAJOR TEAMS: Western Province, Stormers, Sharks, Racing 92

Siya Kolisi made history when he became the first black player to captain the South African national team. Born on 16 June 1991, in Port Elizabeth, Kolisi grew up in poverty and began playing rugby at a young age as a way to escape the challenges of his upbringing. Kolisi's talent was quickly recognised, and he joined the Western Province Rugby Union in 2010, before moving on to play for the Stormers in Super Rugby.

In 2013, Kolisi made his debut for the South African national team, and he quickly became a regular starter. Kolisi's leadership skills were first recognised in 2018 when he was appointed as the captain of the South African national team by coach Rassie Erasmus. Kolisi led the team to a historic victory in the 2019 Rugby World Cup, where they defeated England in the final, with Kolisi playing a crucial role in the victory. Kolisi is known for his powerful ball-carrying ability, his tenacity in defence, and his leadership skills both on and off the pitch.

He has become an inspirational figure in South Africa, especially for young black players who aspire to follow in his footsteps. Kolisi has also been active in promoting social justice and equality in South Africa. He has used his platform to advocate for issues such as racial equality and access to education, and has set up a foundation to support disadvantaged children in South Africa. In 2023 Kolisi became a world champion for a second time when he captained the Springboks in their 12-11 defeat of the All Blacks in the Rugby World Cup final, only the second skipper in history after Richie McCaw to lift the famous trophy twice.

Position	Blindside flanker
Country	South Africa
Test span	2013-
Test caps	92
Test points	60 (12T)

Traiblazer Kolisi is the first black South African captain in the 126 years of the sport

RUGBY LEGENDS

OPENSIDE FLANKERS

The perfect No 7 is a player of many talents, able to support and carry in attack yet tackle ceaselessly and be first on the scene to secure possession at the breakdown. You will push the boundaries of legality and so need the stealth of a cat burglar as you flit around the field stealing the ball without attracting the referee's attention. Although one of the smaller forwards, you should have terrific strength over the ball – and you must never stop! Opensides often make good captains as they are at the heart of the action – there are several great leaders in our list.

QANTAS

THIERRY DUSAUTOIR

Cool blue Dusautoir drives forward at Eden Park

MAJOR TEAMS: Bordeaux-Bègles, Colomiers, Biarritz, Toulouse

Two World Cup ties against New Zealand with a combined total of 52 tackles represent a pair of defining performances from Thierry Dusautoir. Differing results mean the France flanker will hold contrasting memories of each occasion, although both saw him gallop across the line to finish off sweeping attacks.

The first came at Cardiff's Millennium Stadium in 2007 when Richie McCaw's All Blacks were suffocated by an assassin in the No 7 shirt, surrendering a 13-3 half-time lead to go down 20-18.

Dusautoir cut down an incredible 38 carriers that evening, a truly effervescent effort. He hadn't even been named in Bernard Laporte's 30-man squad for the tournament, being drafted in as an injury replacement for Elvis Vermeulen.

Four years on and Dusautoir was captaining les Bleus in a siege of Eden Park. Though France had already lost twice in the pool stages, once to unfancied Tonga, they had a chance to halt the hosts in the final.

Thanks largely to the breakdown disruption of Dusautoir, an upset almost materialised. Without some peculiar ruck interpretations by referee Craig Joubert, Auckland might have been silenced. Dusautoir was named World Player of the Year after the tournament.

Concentrating fully on the game at 16 following a foundation in judo, Dusautoir went from Bordeaux-Bègles to Biarritz via Colomiers before arriving at Toulouse, where he accumulated over 200 appearances, not to mention the 2010 Heineken Cup. His 80 Test caps include 34 in the Six Nations, in which he led France to a Grand Slam in 2010.

Born in the Ivorian city of Abidjan, he's a chemical engineering graduate who penned a resolute response to the 2015 terrorist attack on Charlie Hebdo magazine for the Huffington Post.

Though his compatriots are often labelled as impassioned, Dusautoir has always been clinical.

"Thierry is not prone to rushes of blood to the head," said his old adversary Lewis Moody, the former England captain. "He is very controlled with his emotions, which is why he was such a good leader for France over the years." Dusautoir certainly bore the hallmarks of a focused winner.

Position	Openside flanker
Country	France
Test span	2006-15
Test caps	80 (79 starts)
Test points	30 (6T)

JAN ELLIS

Ellis spark The Boks flanker set new standards in fitness

MAJOR TEAMS: SW Africa, Transvaal

Jan Ellis, the flame-haired flanker from Brakpan, was known as the 'Red Devil' and was fiendishly fit for a player in the amateur era thanks to his habit of running up and down sand dunes carrying bricks.

Ellis is spoken about with almost the same reverence as Frik du Preez, whose record of caps he equalled in 1976 on the day he played his 38th Test, against the All Blacks.

For 11 years from 1965 he missed only one Test – against England in 1969 – and there was a national outcry when the South African selectors called time on his career.

Able to play on either flank, Ellis was a swift back-row with a unique leaning running style. He scored 32 tries in 74 games for the Boks, and his legendary fitness had a lot to do with his longevity. With Piet Greyling and Tommy Bedford, he made up one of South Africa's finest breakaway trios, but he was the quiet man of the three who spurned attention and preferred his own company to attending official functions.

Ellis also had a short fuse and threatened to leave the 1969-70 end-of-year tour to Europe when the team was struggling and he was getting fed up with the dressing-downs from coach Avril Malan.

But Boks fans, particularly from South West Africa (now Namibia), where he was brought up, were prepared to forgive his shortcomings off the field, and there was widespread concern when he was shot in 2000 during an armed robbery at the garage he owned in Pretoria. Ellis was 57 at the time but pulled through, before passing at the age of 71 in 2013.

Oregan Hoskins, the then president of the South African Rugby Union, said, "He was one of those unbelievably tough Springbok forwards for which our country is renowned." Nobody in South Africa would disagree.

Position	Openside flanker
Country	South Africa
Test span	1965-76
Test caps	38 (38 starts)
Test points	21 (7T)

PETER WINTERBOTTOM

MAJOR TEAMS: Headingley, Hawke's Bay, Harlequins

One of England's greatest players of the modern yet amateur era, Winterbottom was a ferocious flanker whose shattering tackling was universally feared. Even by pre-professional standards of stature, he was not a big man but his impact was huge and when he featured in the XV that demolished Ireland at Twickenham in 1992, he became only the second player in history to register 50 appearances for the Red Rose.

First capped against the Wallabies in 1982, the first half of the openside's Test career was hampered by injury but his later rebirth and relentless displays coincided with England's own rejuvenation with Winterbottom an ever-present in the side that registered back-to-back Grand Slams in 1991 and 1992.

At the same time the Red Rose were making their mark on the global stage, reaching their first World Cup final in 1991. Winterbottom featured in five of the six games, including the agonising 12-6 loss to Australia in the final at Twickenham. His England career came to an end against Ireland in Dublin in 1993, his tally of 58 caps for his country at seven a national record which endured for a decade.

His incredible durability, however, was best illustrated by his double selection for the Lions. The back rower was first picked for the 1983 tour of New Zealand at the age of 23 and despite his relative inexperience at international level, started all four Tests against the All Blacks. He missed out on selection for Australia six years later but returned to the squad for the tourists for their return to New Zealand, where he had previously played club rugby for Hawke's Bay, in 1993.

Winterbottom was the only survivor from 1983 to renew hostilities with the All Blacks a decade later, a remarkable study in longevity in an era when players had to balance full-time employment with their playing commitments. The flanker was once again to the fore in all three Tests, including the famous 20-7 victory in Wellington.

In 2005 Winterbottom was inducted to the Twickenham 'Wall of Fame' in recognition of his service to English rugby.

Position	Openside flanker
Country	England
Test span	1982–1993
Test caps	58
Lions caps	7
Test points	13 (3T)

RICHIE MCCAW

MAJOR TEAMS: Crusaders, Canterbury

Even before he had made a national age-grade team, Richie McCaw believed he was going to the top. Encouraged by an uncle while waiting for food to arrive in a McDonald's, the teenage McCaw wrote down a list of rugby goals on a napkin. He was to achieve them all, including becoming an All Black three years ahead of schedule in 2001.

It's funny now to think that his debut in Dublin at the age of 20 on a long-ago autumn tour caused umbrage because McCaw had only played 17 first-class games. The young openside was named Man of the Match that day and went on to break a host of Test records; among them, the most-capped player (148, since overtaken), most caps as captain (109) and most Test tries by a flanker (27).

It's impossible to overstate McCaw's influence in rugby history. An arch turnover merchant with the knack of staying on the right side of referees, he also set the bar in terms of tackle rate, clearing rucks and ball-carrying. His endurance levels were remarkable and his refusal to bow to a foot fracture at the 2011 World Cup – sustained before the knockout stage even began – was heroic.

"He can hardly walk and how he played today I just don't know," said head coach Graham Henry after New Zealand edged past France 8-7 in that year's final. "That he got through it was down to his heart and determination. He's the best leader this country has ever had."

A three-time World Player of the Year, McCaw followed that by lifting the Webb Ellis Cup again in his final match, the defeat of Australia at RWC 2015.

His accomplishments haven't been the sole reserve of the sports field. He once scored 99.4% in a maths exam at Otago Boys High School and other activities include playing the bagpipes and piloting gliders – riding a wave at 20,000 feet is one of his greatest pleasures.

For a player who so regularly soared above the rest, it's only fitting that McCaw now flies helicopters for a living out of Christchurch. It will be a long time before we see his like again.

World in his hands McCaw played through the pain at the 2011 World Cup

Position	Openside flanker
Country	New Zealand
Test span	2001-15
Test caps	148 (141 starts)
Test points	135 (27T)

GEORGE SMITH

On a pedestal Eddie Jones called Smith the greatest player he has ever coached

MAJOR TEAMS: Brumbies, Toulon, Suntory Goliath, Stade Français, Lyon, Wasps, Queensland Reds, Bristol

In the wake of an agonising 27-22 defeat by the Chiefs in the 2013 Super 15 final, Brumbies coach Jake White saluted George Smith. "He's a phenomena," he said. It was easy to forgive the grammatical error. Over the years, Smith certainly seemed like a plural form as he almost single-handedly altered the breakdown landscape.

Signed by Eddie Jones to the Brumbies, he stormed onto the Super Rugby scene as a dreadlocked 20-year-old in 2000, making his debut against the Sharks and scoring a try in the final as the Crusaders won 20-19.

A senior cap in France followed, and 11 months on the Lions were Down Under. Smith's reputation rocketed. He hauled Australia back into contention after defeat in the first Test, celebrating his 21st birthday with a Man of the Match performance in the series-sealing victory in Sydney.

Smith's innovative ability to support his own bodyweight, latch onto the ball and snaffle possession at tackle situations was an indelible feature of the Brumbies' Super Rugby win later that year too, and individual prizes mounted up. Nine Brett Robinson Awards for Brumbies players' player supplemented two John Eales medals. In 2009 he became the youngest man (at that point) to hit 100 Tests when starting against New Zealand aged 29 years and four days.

Smith then took his talents globetrotting to France and Japan, a period that coincided with him being made a Member of the Order of Australia. Tempted back to Australia when the Lions toured in 2013, he starred for the Brumbies, clinching a tenth Brett Robinson gong and earning an 111th outing against Warren Gatland's men.

The Wallabies lost the decider 41-16 and Smith received a sickening head knock when colliding with hooker Richard Hibbard.

But this wasn't farewell for one of the most durable figures in the pro era. Smith was to shine for Lyon, Wasps, Reds and Bristol before retiring at the age of 38.

Ex-Wallabies team-mate Justin Harrison said Smith inspired a whole generation of Australian rugby supporters to play the game. "We are richer for having had the opportunity to witness George playing in a gold Wallaby jersey," he said.

Position	Openside flanker
Country	Australia
Test span	2000-13
Test caps	111 (93 starts)
Test points	45 (9T)

WAVELL WAKEFIELD

English rock Wakefield (left) at the 1924 match versus France

MAJOR TEAMS: Harlequins, Leicester

Nowadays administrators devise the laws and players just play, but there was a time when the lines were distinctly blurred. Wavell Wakefield was challenging the status quo long before he hung up his boots as England's most-capped player – a record he was to retain for 43 years.

A former RAF officer, Wakefield played in three Grand Slam-winning teams in the 1920s, including the 1924 side that he captained. At 14st, he was England's heaviest forward and he was quick with it, as befitting a former 440 yards champion.

More formidable still was the aggression he brought to the field. He once wrote that "it is one of the glories of rugger that you can put your shoulder into a man with all your strength and bring him down with a crash, knowing that if you stave in a rib or two of his he will bear no grudge against you".

He could play at lock, No 8 and even centre, but he makes our list of flying breakaways by virtue of his pioneering influence on the role of the loose forward.

Wakefield brought a new athleticism and tactical element to back-rows, getting them to handle like backs in attack and cover the ground so effectively in defence that the English game was briefly threatened by a try drought.

He was a paradox, staunchly upholding the RFU's amateur principles while adopting a quasi-professionalism in terms of training, fitness and analysis. He abolished the 'first up, first down' scrum dogma forever, giving forwards specialist roles and thereby greater expertise.

At Leicester Tigers, he experimented with a four-man front row and three-man second row, whilst at Cambridge, where he studied engineering, he put numbers on players' jerseys at the Varsity Match.

"He was the rock from which every subsequent back-rower was carved," said social historian Tony Collins, and Wakefield's influence didn't end there. The long-time Conservative MP was Harlequins president for 30 years and served the RFU and IRB (now World Rugby) with distinction.

Position	Openside flanker
Country	England
Test span	1920-27
Test caps	31 (31 starts)
Test points	18 (6T)

JEAN-PIERRE RIVES

MAJOR TEAMS: Toulouse, Racing

If someone mentions the name Jean-Pierre Rives and you don't immediately think of an unruly blond mane atop a bloodied face, something is amiss.

Nicknamed *Casque d'Or* – Golden Helmet – Rives was the star of French rugby in the 1970s and 1980s and became one of those rarities in the world of rugby: a player famous beyond the sport.

Rives captained France a then record 34 times, playing alongside Jean-Claude Skrela and Jean-Pierre Bastiat in a legendary back row. His style was the very essence of what was seen as the typically French mode: gloriously free-spirited, unpredictable and entertaining.

He only wanted to drive a maul to one place – right out of the game. As he once told the *Irish Independent*: "The ball is the star. People want to see the ball. Kids want to see it being passed."

Born in Toulouse on New Year's Eve 1952, Rives was considered too small to be a

Blood sport Rives was the fearless face of French rugby

top-class openside as he never reached 6ft, but his tremendous bravery and seeming ability to be everywhere on the pitch at once saw him win his first cap when he was only 22.

He helped France win a Grand Slam in 1977, led them to arguably their finest-ever victory as they beat New Zealand 24-19 at Eden Park on Bastille Day in 1979, and won a second Grand Slam in 1981.

France's Player of the Year in 1977, 1979 and 1981, Rives was forced into retirement by shoulder problems in 1984, but the honours kept on coming; he was awarded the prestigious Légion d'honneur in 1986 and the National Order of Merit in 2009.

He has found new fame as a sculptor and artist, exhibiting across the world. Google him and you will find as many references to that as to his rugby. "Art is like rugby," he says. "It is all about having a 'feeling' and it is a way of life."

He maintains some connections with the game, as he was involved in the 2007 World Cup in France, and he created the Giuseppe Garibaldi Trophy, which is awarded annually to the winner of the Six Nations match between France and Italy.

Position	Openside flanker
Country	France
Test span	1975-84
Test caps	59 (59 starts)
Test points	20 (5T)

MICHAEL HOOPER

Australian icon Hooper gives the Wallaby supporters a thumbs-up in Perth

MAJOR TEAMS: Brumbies, NSW Waratahs, Toyota Verblitz

It takes a special player to wear a nation's armband at 22, as Hooper did when first being handed the Wallabies captaincy against France in 2014.

The flanker has now done the job a record 65 times while racking up a stream of other bests, including the youngest player to win 100 Super Rugby caps, the fastest to win 50 Test caps, the youngest to win 100 Test caps (until George North beat him by 29 days) and the first Wallaby forward to score 20 Test tries.

He's much more than a classic scavenging seven; he's a thunderous ball-carrier, and does anyone in world rugby cover more ground? At times during his decade-long international career it has felt as if this Sydney-born warrior was carrying all of Australia on his shoulders.

Glasgow's Jack Dempsey, a former team-mate of Hooper, says, "The biggest thing about Hoops is that he can play every week and for 80 minutes. The level he plays at consistently is amazing. He's another level."

Initially at the Brumbies, where he was mentored by George Smith, Hooper was named Rookie of the Season in 2012 and signed for the Waratahs the next season. His courage and tenacity made him an instant favourite.

With an English-born father, who emigrated Down Under at 24, Hooper could have worn the red rose on his chest. Instead, he has been the scourge of England and every other nation, often in tandem with David Pocock, another brilliant back-row who just missed out on our list.

Position	Openside flanker
Country	Australia
Test span	2012-2023
Test caps	125
Test points	110 (22T)

The Aussies know what a gem they possess, awarding him the John Eales Medal (for Australia's Player of the Year) in 2013, 2016 and 2020, and the Matt Burke Cup (Waratahs' best player) on seven occasions.

"It's hard to believe how high his energy levels are," said ex-Lions captain Sam Warburton.

"We all see the eye-catching stuff – the stunning carries, running into front-five forwards, the smart quick taps – but you also have to look at his kick chases, how he works back in defence and the punch and power he provides in a tackle. He's like a pinball machine, bouncing around and always bouncing back up."

In June 2024 he announced his international retirement and turned his attention to sevens rugby, debuting for Australia in the World Series in Hong Kong.

MICHAEL JONES

MAJOR TEAMS: Auckland, Blues

John Hart's barometer for world-beating ability has been unerring. As the New Zealand U21 coach in 1990, it was he who saw something special in a lanky second-row from Leicester, bringing Martin Johnson on tour to Australia.

Five years earlier as Auckland boss in a glittering season that saw National Provincial Championship glory and the beginning of a 61-match Ranfurly Shield defence, Hart handed a 20-year-old openside his NPC debut.

Michael Jones excelled straightway, his pace and comfort on the ball marking him out as a magnificent attacker. Without possession, the awesome power in his wiry frame made for shuddering hits.

Qualifying through his mother, he appeared once for Western Samoa before touring the British Isles with the New Zealand Barbarians.

By 1987 and the inaugural World Cup, Hart had risen to the post of All Blacks assistant coach. He would later label Jones "almost the perfect rugby player" and drafted his protégé into the hosts' squad. The decision was vindicated rapidly.

Jones was the first player to score a World Cup try, darting over on his New Zealand debut 30 minutes into a 70-6 thrashing of Italy. He featured in three more matches, including the triumphant final.

Though a gruesome knee injury sustained against Argentina in 1989 reduced his speed, Jones reinvented himself as a more belligerent performer and influenced at the highest level

Position	Openside flanker
Country	Western Samoa, NZ
Test span	1986-98
Western Samoa caps	1 (1 start)
New Zealand caps	55 (54 starts)
Test points	56 (13T)

The Iceman cometh Jones shrugs off the 1993 Lions

whenever fitness and faith allowed, not least in three consecutive starts during the victorious 1993 Lions series.

Staunch Christian beliefs meant playing on the Sabbath was out of the question – even for the 1991 World Cup semi-final with Australia – and a nickname of 'Iceman' originated due to the number of ice packs that decorated his body.

Finishing with a defeat to the Wallabies in 1998, Jones won just 55 caps over a period in which New Zealand played 90 Tests. Still, his legacy as one of the all-time greats is rock-solid.

FERGUS SLATTERY

MAJOR TEAMS: University College Dublin, Blackrock College

Such was Fergus Slattery's remarkable longevity that he represented Ireland over 15 seasons, winning 61 caps. With an all-court game that would allow him to thrive in the backs if he so chose, it was as a loose forward that he made his name.

Hailing from Dun Laoghaire, he played his schools rugby for Blackrock College, Dublin before graduating to Blackrock RFC and being capped in 1970. He made the following year's British & Irish Lions tour at 22, seeing it as a learning experience as Wales' John Taylor was preferred for the Test series.

Two years later he played a significant part in the epic Barbarians-New Zealand game, scoring in a clash most notable for Gareth Edwards's 'best-ever' try.

By 1974, Slattery was too good to ignore. When the Lions toured South Africa, he beat Tony Neary to a Test spot because of his indefatigable tackling and ability to protect Phil Bennett from marauding Springboks.

His play made a huge impression on team-mate Ian McGeechan: "He underlined the defensive principle I've driven into all the teams I've coached: that the most important defender is the man just inside the ball and just inside you."

After an invincible tour, Slattery was left with one frustration. In the dying embers of the final Test, with the score 13-13, he crossed the line thinking he'd won the series, only for the referee to rule it out.

Slattery led Ireland 18 times, with one of his greatest achievements a first unbeaten tour to Australia and a series win. As well as his fearless work around the fringes, he was feted for his clever link-up play and blistering pace that saw him reaching the opposition centres as fast as the ball.

He won a Triple Crown for Ireland in 1982 as captain before playing his final game against France two years later.

In retirement, Slattery became a successful property developer.

Position	Openside flanker
Country	Ireland
Test span	1970-84
Ireland caps	61 (61 starts)
Lions caps	4 (4 starts)
Test points	12 (3T)

Tireless tearaway "He was like a dog chasing a bone," said one team-mate of Ireland and Lions flanker Slattery

ARDIE SAVEA

MAJOR TEAMS: Wellington, Hurricanes, Kobelco Kobe Steelers, Moana Pasifika

Ardie Savea is a New Zealand rugby union player who is widely regarded as one of the best flankers in the world. Savea's breakthrough season came in 2016 when he made his debut for the New Zealand national team. He played a key role in the team's successful Rugby Championship campaign that year, earning himself the title of the tournament's Best Player.

Savea's skill, agility, and physicality on the pitch have made him one of the most feared flankers in world rugby. He is known for his ability to make powerful runs with the ball, his quick thinking and sharp passing skills, and his tenacity in defence.

In 2019, Savea made headlines when he became the first All Black to wear a protective headgear that incorporated a chinstrap. He wore the headgear as a way to support his cultural identity, as it was designed to resemble a traditional Samoan headband.

Savea was pipped for a leadership role from early in his rugby career, finally being named captain in 2021 for matches against Australia and South Africa. Teammate Beauden Barrett was full of praise for Savea, saying: "He doesn't speak too much but when he does, you certainly listen to him. He's powerful with his words... He's an absolute beast on the field; leads by action – that's what you want as a skipper."

Such high praise doesn't come lightly, and Savea was voted as All Blacks Player of the Year by his peers in 2021, to go along with his World Rugby Player of the Year nomination in 2019.

Savea has also been active in promoting social justice and equality in New Zealand. He has used his platform to advocate for issues such as mental health awareness and racial equality, and has become a role model for many young people in New Zealand and around the world.

Crowned the World Rugby Player of the Year in 2023,, he made history in late 2024 when he touched down against the Wallabies to become the highest try-scoring forward in All Black history with 28.

Position	Openside flanker
Country	New Zealand
Test span	2016-
Test caps	96
Test points	140 (28T)

Barnstormer Savea breaks no sweat as the Wallabies give chase, Bledisloe Cup 2021

AIG
ALL BLACKS
adidas
allblacks.com

RUGBY LEGENDS

NO. 8s

If you want to stay busy, this is the role for you. Ceteris paribus, no player will carry the ball more often than the No 8, and as one of the team's heavyweights you will be expected to make good yardage and offload out of the tackle. As the player controlling the ball after it's hooked in the scrum, the No 8 is a key decision-maker because you can elect to pick it up and run. So good hands are a must, but then pretty much everything isa must for the No 8 because this is one of the all-singing, all-dancing positions – two of our top ten have even dropped a Test-match goal!

WALTER SPANGHERO

MAJOR TEAMS: Narbonne

"Cometh the hour, cometh the man," said French critics when Walter Spanghero made his debut against South Africa in 1964. France were yearning for a heavy, fast back-five forward to strengthen their pack. Spanghero, a last-minute choice, fitted the bill. He was the most mobile forward in an 8-6 victory against a Springbok side that labelled him rugby's quickest 15-stoner.

Spanghero became the automatic choice as second-row partner to Benoit Dauga in the seasons leading to France's historic first Grand Slam in 1968. He might have made our list of locks, but at 6ft 3in he was small for that position and lineout play was not his forte. So we prefer him at No 8, where he switched three years into his Test career.

Broad-shouldered with powerful legs and a lust for the ball, he had all the attributes of a dynamic forward. In the open, he showed he was perfectly suited to the emphasis on second-phase play that laid the foundations for France's Five Nations title in 1967 and Grand Slam the year after.

Ironically, Dauga underwent the same conversion to No 8, and what had been an effective partnership became a bitter rivalry. Spanghero fell out of favour with the national selectors for two years until he was recalled as captain when Dauga was dropped in 1972. Spanghero duly inspired his charges to adopt the expansive approach that France are renowned for and England suffered a spectacular 37-12 defeat.

He was thus welcomed back as a national hero and led France through the unique five-way Championship tie in 1973 before retiring to concentrate on business interests in his beloved Narbonne.

Colin Meads described Spanghero as "that most docile, delightful man off the field, and in a match hard but scrupulously fair". But it was Spanghero's own view – that rugby was nothing without heart – that summed up the philosophy of one of the French game's best-loved characters.

Position	No 8
Country	France
Test span	1964-73
Test caps	51 (51 starts)
Test points	14 (4T)

Change of role Spanghero started out as a second-row

WAYNE SHELFORD

Big Buck Shelford's courage has passed into lore

MAJOR TEAMS: Auckland, North Harbour, Northampton, Roma

When debates rage over the hardest men to ever play rugby union, Wayne 'Buck' Shelford will forever get a mention.

A force at the back of the scrum for the All Blacks, Shelford clawed and thumped his way towards a reputation as an unyielding competitor. His time in Test rugby was short-lived – he amassed just 22 caps – but while there he barged his way into the global game's consciousness, not only winning a World Cup but overseeing a period of Kiwi dominance.

After fine displays for North Harbour in 1985, young Buck toured Argentina, wearing the famous black for the first time against Club Atlético San Isidro in Buenos Aires. A year later he made his full Test debut in France. It was Shelford's second full cap, against the same foes, that has become part of rugby folklore. Playing in the 'Battle of Nantes', a forceful boot aimed at Buck's groin tore his scrotum, with the No 8 also losing several teeth at the bottom of the same ruck. With frightening calm, Shelford asked to be stitched up and sent back out. Eventually he was hauled off, concussed, and the All Blacks lost 16-3, but it would be the only Test he ever lost.

Position	No 8
Country	New Zealand
Test span	1986-90
Test caps	22 (22 starts)
Test points	20 (5T)

In 1987 he was part of the all-conquering New Zealand side that won the inaugural World Cup. The next year he became captain and led the All Blacks on a 14-game unbeaten run. When he was dropped for Zinzan Brooke in 1990, a national campaign began to 'Bring back Buck'.

He never played another Test but Shelford had left his mark on rugby. In the late 1980s he wanted to make a change. Not to his side's play but to the haka. Before Shelford's intervention, the war dance had none of its current brutal majesty, so he taught his peers how to perform Ka Mate right. Perhaps that is his greatest contribution of all.

ZINZAN BROOKE

MAJOR TEAMS: Auckland Blues, Harlequins, Coventry

How many forwards are best remembered for kicking a drop goal? Not many, but the extraordinary kick Zinzan Brooke slotted from almost 50m out during New Zealand's 1995 World Cup semi-final win over England left an indelible imprint on those who saw it.

The three points helped New Zealand win 45-29 and stole a little of the limelight from four-try sensation Jonah Lomu that day.

It was the 31st Test in Brooke's 58-cap career and the dominant role the No 8 was playing in the All Blacks side at that stage disguises the stuttering start he made.

The son of a farmer from near Auckland, Brooke first turned out for the All Blacks against Argentina in June 1987, but had to wait until July 1989 for his second cap as Buck Shelford was still first choice. By 1991 Brooke was firmly established in the New Zealand side and the following year he was joined by brother Robin, who won 62 caps.

Strong and agile, Zinny was a back-row like no other. "He had better kicking and handling skills than some fly-halves playing international rugby," former England captain Will Carling wrote in 2007. "You align that with his strength and ability to read the game – he was unique."

Former All Blacks selector Peter Thorburn echoed those sentiments: "Zinny was a special beast. He would stand in the foyer of a hotel doing tricks and skills. It was like he had grown up with a ball under his arm."

The New Zealander captained Auckland Blues to Super 12 titles in 1996 and 1997, and also played for New Zealand Maori.

Brooke's 1995 drop-goal proved to be no one-off, as he kicked others against South Africa and Wales in ensuing years. The 17 Test tries he scored was a world record for a forward when he won his last cap, against England at Twickenham in 1997.

Brooke stayed on in London, playing for and coaching Harlequins. He turned out for Coventry and then his new hometown club Windsor, where the father of six is still a member and coaches. One of his boys, Lucas, recently signed an academy contract with London Irish. If he enjoys a career half as special as his father's, the Exiles have a serious player on their hands.

Position	No 8
Country	New Zealand
Test span	1987-97
Test caps	58 (54 starts)
Test points	89 (17T, 3DG)

House of Zin Brooke was a forward with the skills of a stand-off

JIM TELFER

Jim class Leading out the Scots for the 1969 Calcutta Cup match

MAJOR TEAMS: Melrose

The son of a Borders shepherd, Jim Telfer is a legend of Scottish rugby on two fronts. As a belligerent back-row, his courage, work-rate and rucking skills made him an automatic choice from his 1964 debut against France onwards.

In only his second Test, he earned the Scots a 0-0 draw against New Zealand by diving on a loose ball near his own line and hanging on for grim death while the All Blacks tried to shoe him to oblivion. Two months later, on his first start at No 8, his try helped to beat England and spark the first pitch invasion seen at Murrayfield.

Telfer trained five times a week – unheard of in the 1960s – in order to gain an edge, and he became a disciple of the ferocious rucking game employed by New Zealand sides of that and many an era.

He played eight British & Irish Lions Tests across the 1966 and 1968 tours, and the late Colin Meads, with whom he was to cross swords on many an occasion, believed Telfer should have captained the first of those tours to his country. "He should have been an All Black forward," he said.

A chemistry teacher by profession, Telfer began coaching in earnest in 1974 and so embarked on a golden second career.

Position	No 8
Country	Scotland
Test span	1964-70
Scotland caps	25 (25 starts)
Lions caps	8 (8 starts)
Test points	9 (3T)

Highlights include coaching Scotland to a first Grand Slam for 59 years in 1984; whipping the Lions pack into shape in 1997 in an infamous session of 60 scrums in half an hour; and securing Melrose's first Scottish Division One title – a success that brought him as much pleasure as any.

Nicknamed 'Creamy' after a Grand National horse of the 1940s that he admired, Telfer coached with the same hard-nosed attitude that he showed as a player, though in his autobiography he took issue with the public perception of him as some sort of "brusque ogre".

Telfer remains the only Scottish international to have played against the big three southern hemisphere giants and not tasted defeat – an epitaph he will probably take to his grave.

JUAN MARTÍN FERNÁNDEZ LOBBE

MAJOR TEAMS: Sale Sharks, Toulon

A treble champion of Europe and part of the backbone of Toulon's star-studded team for six years, Juan Martín Fernández Lobbe is one of Argentina's greatest players.

Versatile enough to have played Test rugby in all three back-row positions and influential enough to have led his country in their first season in the Rugby Championship, this star from Buenos Aires helped Argentina earn and retain their seat at rugby's top table.

Fernández Lobbe played amateur rugby with Liceo Naval in Argentina and completed an engineering degree before moving to England to turn professional with Sale Sharks in 2006 when he was 24. He captained Sale in 2008-09 before he was snapped up by Toulon, with whom he won three successive European Cups.

After playing for Argentina Sevens, Fernández Lobbe won his first Test cap in 2004, following his older brother Ignacio into the Pumas squad. Ignacio retired from Test rugby after the 2007 World Cup with 66 caps – a mark his younger brother overhauled before he retired after leading the Barbarians against England in 2018. "It's my last game ever but I'm at peace," he said.

A tough operator at the breakdown and a powerful defender, Juan Martín read the game brilliantly and popped up in try-scoring positions, netting three in consecutive Tests in 2005-06 against Samoa and Wales (twice).

The forward was a pivotal figure in the Argentina team that claimed bronze at the 2007 World Cup in France – by far and away the Pumas' finest hour to date.

He led Argentina for the first time in 2008, continued as captain in 2009 while Felipe Contepomi was injured, and was at the helm again for the first two Rugby Championship campaigns in 2012 and 2013. In 2009 the then Scotland coach Andy Robinson called Fernández Lobbe "the standout No 8 in the world", and his retirement left a big hole in the Pumas squad.

Position	No 8
Country	Argentina
Test span	2004-15
Test caps	71 (69 starts)
Test points	25 (5T)

Influencer Fernández Lobbe at the 2015 World Cup in England

PAT LAM

MAJOR TEAMS: Auckland, Crusaders, North Harbour, Newcastle, Northampton

Although Auckland-born, Pat Lam is of Samoan descent and is revered on the rugby-mad island. Not only as a teak-tough No 8 who could offload, carry hard and drive attackers backwards but as a leader who helped put Samoa on the rugby map.

Lam played for the All Blacks in an uncapped game in Sydney but made his first big impact in 1991 when, as a fresh-faced 21-year-old on his debut, he was part of a Western Samoa side that shocked the established order with a 16-13 win over Wales in the World Cup. It led one wag to famously quip, "Thank God Wales weren't playing the whole of Samoa."

Lam was to be hugely influential in the 1995 tournament too, where Samoa again exceeded expectations by reaching the last eight.

A grizzled operator in Super Rugby, he moved to the UK in 1997, where he helped Newcastle win the English Premiership and then Northampton the 2000 Heineken Cup after a nail-biting defeat of Munster. His

Island muscle Arm wrestling at a Premiership launch

fourth child was due on the day of the final but arrived early.

By the time Wales faced Samoa at the 1999 World Cup, he was captain of his country and he played a try-scoring part in curbing Welsh optimism with a 38-31 victory,

Position	No 8
Country	Samoa
Test span	1991-99
Test caps	34 (34 starts)
Test points	25 (5T)

again in Cardiff.

Lam returned to Newcastle to finish his career in 2002, his final game coming for the Barbarians against Wales.

He went into coaching, initially working with Scotland, Auckland, the Blues and Samoa. Ian McGeechan called him the "ideal role model" and as a coach Lam's teams have played scintillating rugby, with Connacht achieving an incredible Pro12 title in 2016 and his current club Bristol Bears now on the rise.

MERVYN DAVIES

MAJOR TEAMS: London Welsh, Swansea

Mervyn Davies will be remembered as a Wales and Lions legend for what he achieved during the 1970s.

Had his career not finished so abruptly at 29, on account of a brain haemorrhage incurred in a Swansea-Pontypool cup tie barely a year after he had led Wales to a Grand Slam, his list of achievements would have included captaining the 1977 Lions.

Davies was a magnificent lineout jumper and a great source of ball, either to set up an attack or feed Gareth Edwards with a deft tap down. Physically, at 6ft 5in and with long arms and huge hands, he was on the gangly side but he was hugely effective.

A lifelong friend, Derek Quinnell, commented, "You knew that if you threw it anywhere in his vicinity he would catch it. He was also a masterful tackler and able to wrap up the opposition with ease. Invariably he'd emerge from the bottom of any ruck,

A great eight Davies could tackle teams to a standstill

killing opposition ball and slowing the ball down to help the team."

When people look back at the 1970s, they tend to think of the Welsh backs but the fact 'Merv the Swerve' is mentioned in such rarefied company shows that he bucked the trend. And his Lions record was exemplary: in eight Tests on New Zealand and South African soil in 1971 and 1974, he only lost one, and only nine Tests in 46 if you factor in Wales.

Davies joined London Welsh in 1968 after taking a teaching post near London. As a leader, he was quiet and unassuming, standing out above other captains because he listened as well as he talked.

In 1971 the All Blacks' natural game was for scrum-half Sid Going to break and link with his back row, and Davies was vital to stifling that at source with the Lions. "He stopped us playing," Colin Meads said.

Davies was never bothered about his image but he will forever be linked with that headband and Zapata moustache. He was a giant among men.

Position	No 8
Country	Wales
Test span	1969-76
Wales caps	38 (38 starts)
Lions caps	8 (8 starts)
Test points	7 (2T)

LAWRENCE DALLAGLIO

MAJOR TEAMS: Wasps

It seems strange to say this after his garlanded career, but Lawrence Dallaglio's finest hour was probably the 2004 tour ordeal in New Zealand. England travelled south as world champions and lost the Tests 36-3 and 36-12, yet you shudder to think what the scores would have been without their captain Dallaglio, whose courage and ferocious commitment in a hopeless cause was astonishing.

Dallaglio was never better when the chips were down, a point acknowledged by his former Wasps coach Shaun Edwards. "Like a great heavyweight in a dangerous title fight," he added, "he was at his best when it was all on the line."

England's most-capped No 8 started life in the backs; at Ampleforth, whom he helped to a National Schools Sevens double in 1989, he was a skinny wing/centre, and even his first few appearances for Wasps were as a replacement for England flyer Chris Oti.

Later, he was picked by England coach Jack Rowell as a No 7 ahead of Neil Back, but in time he found his niche as a six or eight – and he played magnificently in both those positions for the 1997 British & Irish Lions.

Dallaglio was a classic ball-carrier, often the man to truck it up after receiving the kick-off, and as well as his fiery competitiveness and skills from the base of the scrum he possessed a huge engine. He was the only Englishman to play every minute of RWC 2003, when he added a winner's medal to the sevens equivalent collected in 1993. Only he and Matt Dawson have achieved this prize double.

Dallaglio once lost the England captaincy after a scurrilous tabloid sting, yet it speaks volumes that such a high-profile fall from grace is all but forgotten; that's not just down to his achievements but the heart-on-sleeve passion with which he represented both his country and family, including the sister he tragically lost in a ferry disaster when he was 17. He's now a BT Sport pundit.

Position	No 8
Country	England
Test span	1995-2007
England caps	85 (73 starts)
Lions caps	3 (3 starts)
Test points	85 (17T)

Proud to wear the rose Dallaglio was inducted into the World Rugby Hall of Fame in 2016

SERGIO PARISSE

MAJOR TEAMS: Benetton Treviso, Stade Français, Toulon

Few current players are as universally admired as Sergio Parisse, whose handling skills, powerful athleticism and undying determination have lit up the majority of Italy's 21st-century performances.

His parents are Italian but he was born in Argentina while his father (also called Sergio) worked there. Sergio senior had played for L'Aquila and Sergio junior started out with La Plata before transplanting his Italian roots to Treviso in his late teens. He was still three months short of his 19th birthday when Italy coach John Kirwan handed him his first Test cap in June 2002.

Three years later the all-round talent of this 6ft 5in back-row prompted Stade Français to sign him, and he has blossomed ever since. By the age of 24 Parisse had 50 caps and the Italian captaincy to his name, having taken over the helm from Marco Bortolami.

Today only two men have won more Test caps than the 38-year-old and, fitness permitting, he hopes to add to his record 69 Six Nations appearances before retiring at the end of the 2021-22 season. "There are enough examples in his illustrious career that he can pull rabbits out of the hat," said Paul Gustard, the former England defence coach now working at Benetton.

A rare blemish on his record came in 2009 when he was banned for eight weeks for gouging, but the positives far outweigh the negatives for a player who has twice been shortlisted for the World Rugby Player of the Year award – in 2008 and 2013. He has captained the Barbarians and Stade Français, leading them to the French title in 2015. Strong in defence, reliable in the lineout and not adverse to launching a touch-finder or drop-goal, he's best known for his deft and devastating offloads. "He's awesome," said Billy Vunipola, a fellow No 8 of similar pedigree. "He's been at international level for so long and he's so comfortable in that shirt. He can afford to throw those cheeky little balls out of the back door."

Parisse's achievements are all the more remarkable for playing in a struggling team, having lost 106 of his 142 Tests. His ability to soak up the recurring pain of defeat and come back for more is something to marvel at. He retired from international rugby in 2019 and won the EPCR Challenge Cup Final with Toulon in 2023, retiring from rugby after the match.

Power Serge Parisse out jumps Wales full-back Leigh Halfpenny

Position	No 8
Country	Italy
Test span	2002-2019
Test caps	142 (139 starts)
Test points	83 (16T, 1DG)

KIERAN READ

MAJOR TEAMS: Canterbury, Crusaders, Toyota Verblitz

Death, taxes and Kieran Read unpicking defences in the 15m channel – these are three inevitabilities in this world.

Athleticism and on-field intelligence brought Read an All Blacks debut at Murrayfield in 2008, two months after his 23rd birthday. Only two years earlier he had made a provincial bow for Canterbury.

Growing up on New Zealand's North Island before pursuing rugby opportunities across the Cook Strait, Read starred for Karaka Cricket Club close to Auckland. By 16, he was an age-group international batsman. The oval ball won out, however, and Read became a regular in the Crusaders outfit. Starting the victorious 2008 decider against the Waratahs at blindside, Read won a place on the European tour and never looked back.

That Scottish assignment came wearing six too, but by the end of 2009 he was entrenched as Graham Henry's first-choice No 8. Accolades continued with a late try to clinch a 23-22 victory over Australia the next season, sealing the Tri-Nations title and a New Zealand Player of the Year gong.

Glory at the 2011 World Cup foreshadowed a phenomenal 2013. In June, captaining his country in the absence of Richie McCaw, Read oversaw a 30-0 defeat of France in his 50th, and New Zealand's 500th, Test. The year would end with 14 consecutive wins for the All Blacks, and their talisman featured in 13 of them, contributing six tries. He was a runaway World Player of the Year.

While concussion issues surfaced later in his career, lineout prowess and deft link play still set Read apart. He finished as the fourth most-capped All Black, leading them 52 times, and racked up four Super Rugby titles to go with two World Cups. He had a season in Japan's Top League, retiring after Verblitz's semi-final defeat in May 2021. As for the respect of fellow greats, Lawrence Dallaglio once heralded him "better than Buck Shelford and Zinzan Brooke". There is no higher praise.

Position	No 8
Country	New Zealand
Test span	2008-19
Test caps	127 (120 starts)
Test points	130 (26T)

Leading the haka Read achieved an 86% win rate across his All Blacks career

adidas
AIG
AIG
AIG